ABOUT THE AUTHOR

Born in Hamilton, Ontario, in 1955, Cope attended the University of Waterloo, graduating with a B.Sc. in Earth Sciences in 1978. He came to Calgary that same year to work in the oil patch, but his love for writing led him to freelance journalism and a career as a feature writer and business reporter. In 1993, Cope and his wife, Linda, quit their jobs, sold their house, and ran away to the South Pacific. Since then, they have lived in London and Paris and travelled around the world. This book is a result of their year in Paris (2001–2002). They currently live in Calgary with their cat China.

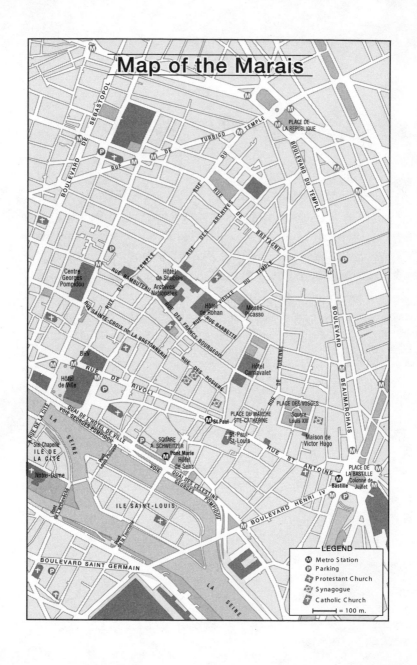

Map of the Marais

PLACE DE LA RÉPUBLIQUE

BOULEVARD DE SEBASTOPOL

RUE DE TURBIGO

RUE DU TEMPLE

BOULEVARD DU TEMPLE

RUE DES ARCHIVES

RUE DE BRETAGNE

RUE VIEILLE DU TEMPLE

Centre Georges Pompidou

RUE RAMBUTEAU

Hôtel de Soubise
Archives Nationales

Hôtel de Rohan

Musée Picasso

RUE SAINTE-CROIX DE LA BRETONNERIE

RUE DES FRANCS-BOURGEOIS

RUE BARBETTE

BHV

RUE DE RIVOLI

RUE DES ROSIERS

Hôtel Carnavalet

RUE DE TURENNE

BOULEVARD BEAUMARCHAIS

Hôtel de Ville

QUAI DE L'HÔTEL DE VILLE
VOIE GEORGES POMPIDOU

PLACE DES VOSGES

PLACE DU MARCHÉ STE-CATHERINE

Square Louis XIII

St-Paul

Ste-Chapelle
ÎLE DE LA CITÉ

Notre-Dame

LA SEINE

SQUARE A. SCHWEITZER

Pont Marie
Hôtel de Sens

St-Paul-St-Louis

RUE ST ANTOINE

Maison de Victor Hugo

PLACE DE LA BASTILLE
Colonne de Juillet

Bastille

VOIE
QUAI DES CELESTINS
GEORGES POMPIDOU

ÎLE SAINT-LOUIS

BOULEVARD HENRI IV

BOULEVARD SAINT GERMAIN

LA SEINE

LEGEND

- Ⓜ Metro Station
- Ⓟ Parking
- Protestant Church
- Synagogue
- Catholic Church

⊢———⊣ = 100 m.

To: Bev & Craig:

May all your moments
be Paris Moments!

A PARIS MOMENT

GORDON COPE

To Bev & Craig:
Much love &
friendship
Linda

FIFTH HOUSE

Cover design by David Drummond
Cover photograph, River Seine, Paris, France, by Yann Layma, Getty Images
Interior design by Kathy Aldous-Schleindl
Edited/copyedited by Liesbeth Leatherbarrow
Proofread by Kirsten Craven
Map by Articulate Eye

The publisher gratefully acknowledges the support of The Canada Council for the Arts and the Department of Canadian Heritage.

THE CANADA COUNCIL | LE CONSEIL DES ARTS
FOR THE ARTS | DU CANADA
SINCE 1957 | DEPUIS 1957

We acknowledge the financial support of the Government of Canada through the Book Publishing Industry Development Program (BPIDP) for our publishing activities.

Printed in Canada by Friesens

05 06 07 08 09/ 5 4 3 2 1

First published in the United States in 2006 by
Fitzhenry & Whiteside
121 Harvard Avenue, Suite 2
Allston, MA 02134

Library and Archives Canada Cataloguing in Publication
Cope, Gordon, 1955-
          A Paris moment / Gordon Cope.
ISBN 1-894856-83-X

1. Cope, Gordon, 1955- --Travel--France. 2. Marais (Paris, France)
3. Marais (Paris, France)--Description and travel. 4. Paris (France)--Description and travel. I. Title.

DC705.C67A3 2005   944'.361084   C2005-902385-6

Fifth House Ltd.
A Fitzhenry & Whiteside Company
1511, 1800-4 St. SW
Calgary, Alberta T2S 2S5

1-800-387-9776
www.fitzhenry.ca

CONTENTS

To my wife Linda, for her love and support.

ACKNOWLEDGEMENTS

I am grateful to the people of Paris, and particularly the Marais, for their willingness to tell their stories and share their lives with a curious Canadian. I am also indebted to those who composed a myriad of sources, including *Tourist Guide Paris* (Michelin Tyre Public Limited Company, 6th Edition), *DK Eyewitness Travel Guides Paris* by Alan Tillier (Dorling Kindersley, 1993), and *A la Découverte du Marais* (Association pour la sauvegarde et la mise en valeur du Paris historique, 1997).

I also wish to thank French history scholar Mark Meyers for reading the manuscript from an historic perspective and Liesbeth Leatherbarrow for editing the manuscript.

JUILLET

A summer storm is imminent and, as we hurry along rue Vieille du Temple, tiny dust devils dance beside us on the pavement like scruffy dogs. We scurry past the park adjacent to the Picasso Museum and make it to the restaurant entrance, just as the first raindrops pound down on the hot July asphalt.

Earlier in the evening, we had passed À 2 pas du Dos, a charming restaurant just around the corner from our apartment on rue Barbette. The front wall, a series of hinged wood-and-glass panels, had been accordioned back to open the interior to the street, and tabletop candles glowed invitingly in its dark recesses. The menu posted by the front door guaranteed gustatory paradise in three courses.

We stand inside the doorway for a moment, peering at our surroundings. The decor is a modern blend of minimalist furniture and semi-abstract paintings of well-endowed centaurs. The maître d', sporting a rakish set of sideburns, escorts us to a table and introduces us to Adonis, our waiter for the evening. For an *apéritif*, Adonis recommends their house specialty, Kir Royale, a mix of crème de cassis liqueur and champagne. Perfect, we decide. If we can't paint the town red we can at least go for a purplish blue. Flashing a brilliant set of Attic teeth, Adonis bustles off to the bar with our order.

While we wait, we survey our surroundings. Casually glancing over the tops of our menus, we admire the nipple rings visible through the mesh T-shirts of the two men sitting beside us. Across the aisle, a very mature businessman in dark glasses is entertaining a very curvy young blonde. Near the door, a party of women with sensibly shaved heads are feeding a golden Labrador retriever bread sticks beneath their table. Adonis arrives and, with a flourish, deposits two champagne flutes on our table. We raise our glasses and toast our move to Paris.

Linda and I had been to the city of lights many times before as visitors and had always enjoyed the restaurants, museums, cafés, and stores. But only in our wildest dreams did we ever imagine *living* here—that was for millionaires and glamorous people in celebrity magazines.

Sometimes, fate delivers your dreams on a silver platter. In the middle of June, Linda received a call from Orlin, the manager of a big American firm based in Houston.

"How would you like to work for a year in Paris?"

"You mean Paris, Texas?"

"Hell, no," he boomed. "Paris, France."

It took Linda a moment to find her voice. "Do you need a decision right now?"

"Course not, Honey. Take a week to think about it."

We spent the next seven days in a state of giddy dread. We knew that an international assignment, even in a city as wonderful as Paris, was no promenade in the *parc*; there would always be obstacles.

Of all the possible problems that might arise, speaking French was right there at the top of the list. I grew up in a town where children were arbitrarily punished with compulsory French lessons. Madame Laglace was a hatchet-faced woman who would order us to conjugate verbs for a half-hour every morning until she could stand it no more and harangue us in a salty French that we were never able to locate in our primers.

After two years of suffering, I was released from Madame Laglace's ministrations and fled to senior high school where, through the kind of luck experienced by passengers on the *Titanic*, I was assigned to her husband, Monsieur Laglace. Although he struggled manfully to pound the niceties of French into my thick skull, the highlight of five years of lessons was my ability to order a peanut-butter-and-banana sandwich.

Not that I was afraid of going to a country where I did not comprehend the language—I once spent a year in Australia—but there are strict laws in France against abusing the language. My version of French went way past abuse, more into the area of aggravated assault. I envisioned the language police pulling me over to the curb and forcing me to speak into a voice ana lyzer to confirm that I was well over the limit of tolerance. I would then be cuffed and hauled before a magistrate who would sentence me to four more years with Madame Laglace. Would I risk going to Paris for that?

A second concern was the matter of documentation. Linda needed to start the job immediately, and such niceties as work visas would have to wait until a later date. The agreement was that she would be hired as a consultant through our company in Calgary and merely be stationed in Paris on a temporary basis, but this was a flimsy fig leaf in the official eyes of Gallic bureaucracy. Would we have to travel to France on the under-carriage of the Concorde?

But these were minor quibbles when compared to the magic of Paris. Several years ago, we stayed at a renovated convent on the Ile Saint-Louis, an island in the middle of the Seine. Each morning, after dining on a buffet of espresso and croissants in the tiny breakfast crypt, we would venture forth to explore the city. The weather was sunny and warm, the food was sublime, and the people we met were gracious to the verge of embarrassment.

One night we ate in the basement of a tiny restaurant around the corner from our hotel. The veal had been cooked to the point where it literally fell apart with a fork. The *jus*, made from cream, bouillon, and Pernod liqueur, was the tastiest sauce that had ever passed between my lips. After the meal, we walked down to the shore of the Seine. On our right, Notre-Dame was ablaze with spotlights; to the east, the full moon rose over the river. I held Linda in my arms and kissed her—it was one of the most beautiful and romantic moments I had ever experienced.

Not that Paris was ceaselessly wonderful. The next time we went, we suffered a hectic kaleidoscope of snooty waiters and kamikaze drivers. Once, while staying in a hotel in La Défense, I made the mistake of going for a haircut. The barber, wearing a tiny black T-shirt and a bolt through his belly button, shaved my hair and beard back to the stubble point favoured by his personal hero, Yasser Arafat. After we finally escaped, we vowed never to come back.

I understand this is typical. On one visit to Paris you are smothered in a *joie de vivre* that literally warms your heart, and on the next, you are treated with all the courtesy normally reserved for a Panzer tank division—and there is no predicting which reception you are going to receive.

As an absolute last resort, we decided to ask our friends for advice.

"Are you nuts?" exclaimed Marge, a long-time friend and

francophobe. "Those Frogs will steal the gum off the sole of your boots and sell it back to you as snails."

Brendan, our Irish friend with a fondness for everything cultural and alcoholic, had a different point of view. "I'd give up Guinness for a year in Paris."

But the deciding word came from Phil, sitting at home thinking about the malignant growth in his brain and all of the wonderful things left undone. "If you don't go, you'll regret it for the rest of your life."

Well, you can't argue with that.

Everyone has a vision of the perfect Paris, one that has been culled from movies, and books, and visits. For me, it consists of the displays of pastry in the windows of corner bakeries, a busker playing the accordion on a bridge over the Seine, a florist sprinkling petals from a bucket of old roses on the sidewalk.

Reality, alas, sucks. Paris is a huge metropolis spread out over hundreds of square kilometres. It is big, noisy, and dirty. As we searched for the perfect place to live through the various *arrondissements*, or districts, of Paris, we soon realized the difficulty of our task. How were we going to find that Paris of our dreams, a neighbourhood that combined access to the delights of a big city with the quiet charm of a rural village?

The list of possibilities was short, and not too sweet. La Défense is modern, open, clean, and close to Linda's work. But it was also built in the seventies to serve as a business centre for France's expanding economy. The massive apartment blocks that dot its landscape have about as much charm as a charity hospital, but without the quality of food.

The Champs-Elysées forms the centre of the 8th

arrondissement, a wide, attractive boulevard running from Napoleon's Arc de Triomphe to the place de la Concorde, adjacent to the Louvre. Swank hotels are outnumbered only by luxury shoe shops where, every weekend, countless women abandon their husbands for the intimate embrace of Charles Jourdan. Needless to say, if you don't own at least one sheikhdom, you go barefoot.

The Left Bank, once the haunt of Hemingway and Sartre, is less expensive, but less, well, French. McDonald's hamburgers, Jeep Cherokees, and *USA Today* news boxes dominate the streets. You are far more likely to hear the pros and cons of *The Sopranos* than existentialism being discussed at the sidewalk tables of Café de Flores.

Only one possibility remained. Years ago, on a brief stopover in Paris, we stayed at a tiny inn on the Right Bank, in the Marais district, the centre for gay Paris and the historical Jewish ghetto. The Hôtel Acacias was barely 3.5 metres wide at street level, but it burrowed up through a sixteenth-century apartment block, a rabbit warren of cubbyholes, dormers, and cul-de-sacs. Whenever we ventured forth onto the rue des Archives, we were greeted by men in Lycra tops and shiny purple work boots, Hassidic Jews in black coats and fedoras, and swarthy Moroccans wheeling immense barrels of briny olives down back lanes. Beautiful women in designer dresses sat with their leather-clad boyfriends at sidewalk cafés. A cacophony of bells rang the hour from crumbling church steeples. It was ancient, it was magic, and, quite frankly, it was weird.

When we returned home, I looked up the history of the Marais. Once upon a time, the neighbourhood was home to wealthy kings, beautiful princesses, and inspired poets. It also sheltered adulterous queens, ruthless dukes, and infamous felons. Civil wars, literary masterpieces, treachery, and liberty were all plotted and hatched here. For a brief time in history, the Marais was a fairytale kingdom and an evil sanctuary, a greenhouse of flowering intellectualism and a haven for evil-doers. It was a neighbourhood rich in controversy and conspiracy, culture, and madness.

In other words, it sounded like our kind of place.

At the invitation of a rental agent, we take a cab and make our way up rue Vieille du Temple to rue Barbette, a tiny lane near the Picasso Museum, to view an apartment for lease. The street, about one hundred metres long, is lined with tall, narrow apartments. The taxi lets us out in front of a set of blue double doors marked with the number 23.

We stand back and take a good hard look at the façade, which, to put it charitably, would make even the most hardened Victorian orphan blush. The building is about three hundred years old, judging from the paint job. The wooden window shutters are hanging at angles that only Salvador Dali would appreciate, and some graffiti goon has sprayed a swirl of black acrylic pornography across the front door. I am reluctant to turn the doorknob with a bare hand, but finally screw up the courage to enter.

The foyer of the building perfectly matches the exterior. A large green garbage bin partially blocks the passageway, and the cobblestones beneath our feet are so old you can still see the gouges made by horseshoes. The musty smell that hangs in the air makes me wonder what else the horses might have left behind.

We are reluctant to go any farther, but the rental agent comes clattering down the wrought-iron circular staircase and kisses us on both cheeks. Monique pats her hairdo and confidently assures us that the trip upstairs is well worth the effort. The apartment, she explains, has been renovated and decorated by the Maestro, an Italian conductor of great distinction, and he has given her instructions to show it only to the most discerning clientele. Never able to resist a little flattery, we follow her up the stairs and enter the apartment.

As Monique promised, the interior has indeed been given the once-over. The plaster walls sport a shiny coat of white paint, and the galley kitchen has been upgraded with modern appliances. But it is the living room that seals the deal. Its ceiling soars five metres above the hardwood floors, and an immense sandstone fireplace covers one wall. Two floor-to-ceiling windows open to the south, and a large, wrought-iron chandelier hangs in the centre of the room.

We sign the lease on the spot. It's a little pricey at 13,000 francs a month, but there's no getting around the charm. I hug Linda in delight. For the next year, this will be our home.

Several days later, when we arrive with our belongings, the graffiti has been scrubbed off the outside of the building and the foyer has been given a thorough cleaning. Any lingering doubts we might have had over our new home vanish.

After we unpack our bags, I examine the apartment more closely. The bedroom is tucked in the back, away from the street noise, which I notice tends to rise to the level of a circus act on occasion, and the bathroom is outfitted with a walk-in shower stall and a claw-foot tub large enough for bathing an ox. Thankfully, there is more than enough space in the living room for me to set up a writing desk, and the dining-room table is large enough to seat eight guests uncomfortably.

The furnishings are another matter. The living room

contains a buffalo-hide lounge chair and the propeller from a Sopwith Camel biplane. In the dining room, hanging above the table, is a large wildlife portrait of what appears to be a cross between a duck and a constipated stork. At noon, when we sit down to lunch, it hovers over the table, staring balefully down at our tuna sandwiches. But these are minor inconveniences, details that can be rectified with a little judicial use of closet space.

That evening, as we sit drinking our Kir Royales in A 2 pas de Dos, we begin to plan how we can turn this apartment into our own home. Here some throw cushions for colour, there a sideboard to hold the stereo, and perhaps a few new pictures to break up the expanse of white walls.

Our appetizers, preceded by a waft of Adonis's cologne, soon arrive. The ravioli, stuffed with artichokes and sprinkled with fresh coriander and smoked bacon, are served in a bowl of beef broth. The seafood is calamari laced with goat cheese, anchovies, and herbs. Both are perfectly spiced and exquisitely presented.

For the main course, Adonis arrives with a lovingly prepared roast rack of lamb. The meat is served with a plate of vegetables that includes fava beans, courgettes, asparagus, and roast onions and garlic cloves, each item prepared separately, then all mixed together. I once saw a wildlife documentary in which a school of piranha picks the bones of a gnu clean in thirty seconds, and I have no doubt whatsoever the piranhas would have been impressed with our efforts. We pause only to gulp down an occasional mouthful of the house red before our plates are licked entirely clean. Thank goodness we didn't order the gnu.

For dessert, the chef prepares roasted figs in homemade ice cream and chocolate cake with a hot fudge centre. By the time we are done, I cannot eat another fig. We thank the staff volubly and are bowed back out onto the street with kisses and handshakes.

By now, the storm has blown over, and a full moon peeks over the Picasso Museum. As we walk home, arm-in-arm, a warm breeze blows up the road, carrying with it the smell of summer asphalt, rain, and urine. Revellers drift up rue Vieille du Temple toward the bars and clubs at the heart of the Marais, but we decide to call it an early night so we can get a good sleep. We are excited about discovering what lies in store for us when we venture out tomorrow.

Our morning coffee is interrupted by the sound of the apartment buzzer. When I open the door, a young man in a blue coverall waves a long-handled brush and asks if I could use a good scrubbing.

It takes me a moment to realize that he is referring to scrubbing our chimney. "No, that's not necessary, I don't use the fireplace."

Undeterred, he holds up a greasy black finger and cheerfully wags it back and forth. "Well, you must clean it once a year anyway. It's the law."

I decide to take his judgment to a higher authority. Every apartment in Paris has a caretaker, or *gardien*. Most live in a tiny apartment near the front door and are responsible for keeping the building clean and ensuring its safety. Ours lives at the top of the spiral staircase. Locking the door behind me, I escort the young man upstairs to consult her.

Our *gardienne*, Madame Greco, turns out to be a tiny Spanish woman with short black hair and a cherubic face. She smiles broadly when I introduce myself and shakes my hand.

"Welcome! Is there something you need?"

I explain that this young man has come to clean my chimney, and Madame Greco's expression changes like a storm passing across the Bay of Biscayne. My pedestrian French is left behind by the torrent that spills forth, but her tone and the fact that the chimney sweep immediately flees down the stairwell at a full gallop are more than enough to give me the general gist of the conversation.

As soon as the young man has gone, Madame Greco calms down and explains the situation. "Watch out for those chimney sweeps," she warns me. "Some are not real *ramoneurs*. They come to check out a home for their gang."

According to Madame Greco, home burglary in Paris is a growth industry. There are *rat caves* who break into wine cellars and steel valuable vintages, and *voleurs* who scale outside walls and enter through open windows on upper floors. And some gangs employ scouts, in the guise of phony chimney sweeps. When they spot a likely victim, they chalk out a sign near the building's front entrance to signal their compatriots in crime. Every conscientious *gardien* periodically checks the front entrance and washes off any suspicious markings.

I thank Madame Greco and return to my apartment. As I reach the doorway, Linda is heading out for her first day on the job. My assignment is to get the house in order and shop for the evening's meal. I kiss her goodbye and head to the kitchen to inspect my new culinary domain.

In addition to being proficient with tools and other manly objects, I am the cook in the family. I love to try new recipes and can chop up ingredients without causing major damage to extremities. Linda considers me useful enough to keep around.

Just before leaving for Paris, I had discovered a recipe for filet mignon in Madeira sauce that is to be our evening's meal.

Checking the larder, I find several jars of spices lurking. The salt and pepper appear fine, but the cumin has last been used to whip up a curry dip for Attila the Hun.

Most of the utensils are tucked away on open shelves built into the wall, which helps my inventory effort. In addition to a motley assortment of pots and pans, there is a Crock-Pot still bearing remnants of the Last Supper. I drag it out from its hiding spot and place it in a cupboard in the hallway, well out of harm's way.

Opening the cutlery drawer, I discover that our predecessors had managed to melt a dimple into the plastic handle of every fork. The cutting knife looks as though it has been used to hammer nails, and the spatula sports a fine patina of dried egg. There is, I conclude, some room for improvement. I draw up an extensive grocery list, placing scouring pads and industrial-strength dish cleaner prominently at the top. Grabbing my backpack, I descend the circular staircase to the foyer.

No sooner do I pass through the large double front doors of our apartment building than I literally bump into a man wearing a black silk top hat. He also sports a morning coat and a rabbit shawl, which I imagine is a little warm for this time of year.

After I apologize for stepping on his creamy white spats, the man introduces himself as Fabien, a tenor in an orchestra that performs in churches around Paris. He hands me a bill card advertising the month's engagements and offers to introduce me to a man who is a magician with a sewing machine, should I ever need a lined velvet cape. At the moment, I am more interested in locating some nice steak. Fabien points me in a northerly direction, towards rue de Bretagne. I thank him and continue on my way.

The corner of rue de Bretagne is marked by a café where several patrons are perched at tiny, scarred round tables jammed onto the narrow sidewalk, their noses buried in newspapers and racing forms. I pick my way through a maze of reclining dogs and cigarette haze toward a forlorn row of second-hand clothing stores, discount kitchenware shops, and a rather frazzled open-air market in which an Algerian greengrocer tries to convince me, unsuccessfully, that the fruit with wrinkly, dusty skin is a special peach from Alsace and not simply something he found in a garbage bin.

Trusting Fabien's judgment, I follow the aroma of roasting chickens until it eventually leads me to a red awning marked *Savoy, Boucher*. Outside, a dozen *poulets* turn on a portable rotisserie; inside, a large meat counter beckons.

Butcher shops in Paris are a carnivore's paradise. The display case is lined with enticing cuts of pork, beef, poultry, and lamb. A gigantic baron of beef nestles adjacent to a pink Breton ham. Tiny lamb chops, each one trimmed and decorated with a tinfoil cap on the end of the bone, recline adjacent to veal stuffed with prunes and ground meat.

Savoy, the *artisan boucher*, a hefty, red-faced man in a stained apron, is wielding a large cleaver with precision and force. I respectfully wait until he has reduced a haunch of pork to its constituent chops before interrupting. "Do you have filet of beef?"

"We certainly do." The butcher leans forward and taps a Polaroid snapshot of a cow taped to the counter. "How does Charolais suit you?"

I gaze down upon the portrait of a contented cow munching on what is undoubtedly non-genetically-modified hay, and gladly order five hundred grams, barbecue cut. Savoy takes a handsome slab of filet out of the display case and, with great zeal, cuts, cleans, and wraps two appetizing portions in less than a minute. Instead of giving me the meat, however, he hands a slip of paper across the counter and points me toward the till.

Behind the till dwells Madame Savoy. Resting one plump hand protectively upon the ancient cash register, she peers at me with an eye that has seen more than its fair share of deadbeat customers. Taking the paper from my hand, she performs a quick calculation and demands 90.10 francs. As luck would have it, I have precisely 90 francs. I offer to pay by credit card, but Madame Savoy sternly points to a sign indicating the minimum charge is 100 francs. Turning my pockets inside out to demonstrate my predicament, I ask if perhaps they could trim a chunk worth 10 centimes off the steak?

Madame Savoy pulls a smoked sausage stick from a blue ceramic jar and points it at me. "What am I going to do with a 10-centime steak? Sell it to a fly?" Her husband suggests that, since I am a new customer, they might forgo the piddling amount until next time, but Madame will have none of it.

I stand there, not sure what to do. The rest of the customers stare at me as if I am something that has just crawled out of a drainpipe. I just should have turned on my heel and fled, but the steaks are too good to pass up, and the thought of a hefty meat monger chasing me down the street with a sausage stick is too awful to contemplate. In the end, I walk back home, dig under the couch pillows until I find a shiny 10-centime piece, then return to claim my dinner.

That evening, I greet Linda at the door with a kiss and a glass of red wine. As she sits at the kitchen counter and supervises, I chop up a cup of shallots and mushrooms, then fry them in butter with a teaspoon of fresh thyme. Setting the shallots and mushrooms aside, I take a deep-bottomed pan and pour in a cup of Madeira wine and a cup of beef bouillon. I reduce this to half and then add a cup of cream, heating the sauce until it thickens. Next, I add the shallots and mushrooms to the sauce and set the mixture aside.

Parisians, preferring their meat grilled, have come up with an ingenious stove-top solution for grilling. From the pantry, I pull a square, shallow pan with a ridged bottom that holds meat a few millimetres above the cooking surface. I cook the two steaks for three minutes a side, until they are *saignant*, or rare. Placing the steaks on a platter, I smother them with the mushroom and shallot sauce and serve them with baby potatoes garnished with coriander.

After the meal, we go for a walk. The evening air is hot, but dry. We follow a slow, southerly course, zigzagging along the narrow streets. We pass a corner brasserie, Camille's, where a waiter in a white apron, black vest, and bow tie carries glasses of red Brouilly out to the tables on the sidewalk. Turning onto the rue des Francs-Bourgeois, we come to the Hôtel Carnavalet, home to the Paris city museum. The ancient mansion has been carefully preserved, right down to the formal garden in the central courtyard. It looks as though the heavy iron gates might swing open at any moment for a coach-and-four to roll forth.

We follow a street cleaner down rue Pavée. The water truck has a large pressure hose attached to a pivot on top and, as the driver slowly advances down the street, an assistant moves from side to side, hosing down the sidewalks. Hassidic Jews in black hats and long coats carefully pick their way around the crew, trying to keep their shoes dry.

We reach rue de Rivoli, a major thoroughfare. In contrast to the narrow streets around our home, it is a wide commercial boulevard lined with wine shops, shoe stores, and bric-a-brac emporiums. Towering over the shops is the immense, grimy façade of Saint-Paul–Saint-Louis church. Just up the street is the Bastille, the birthplace of the Revolution. As we stand amid the tourist buses, greengrocers, and bustle of Marais citizens, I am struck by the immediateness, *the now*, of my surroundings, amid centuries of history. The Marais lives and breathes. *This*, I realize, is Paris.

I decide that I need to learn more about my new neighbourhood and the next morning I head for the W. H. Smith bookstore across from the Louvre. After picking up the *Guide Michelin* and *Eyewitness* travel guide to Paris, I stop and ask a clerk where I might find the literary section on Paris. An American woman, with blonde hair pulled back to show off the brown roots, overhears me speaking English and approaches.

"Howareya?" she asks, sticking out her hand. "My husband Lou and me are from Buffalo. What part of the States are you from?"

"The Canadian part."

"Hah!" She gives me a smile of big white teeth, like a shark to a seal. "I got a friend in Toronto named Tom. He's a dancer. You know him?"

"I know a Tom in Toronto, but he has no feet."

She pauses for a moment. "No, must be another Tom. So, this your first time in Paris?"

"Actually, I live here."

"Really!" This strikes her as something novel, almost bizarre. "What do you *do*?"

"I'm a writer. I'm thinking of doing a book about a year in Paris."

"No kiddin'! You'd better read this!" She pulls a book off a shelf. It is a memoir written by a journalist on assignment from an American magazine. The blurb on the back explains that "the author has set out to enjoy the storied existence of an American in Paris in the grand tradition of Stein, Hemingway, Baldwin, and Liebling." Well, then. No point enjoying Paris in a mediocre tradition, is there? I turn to the first page and I immediately discover that there are two kinds of travellers: those who simply observe and those who use preconceived notions to interact with the locals. I bet that's always appreciated.

I once saw a student from UCLA upbraid an old woman in Malaysia because she was tossing the contents of a night bucket into an open ditch beside the road. "You know what's wrong with your country?" he shouted. "You don't have any proper sewers!"

The old woman looked at him as if he was crazy. Did he think she threw crap into an open ditch because it was fun? She shook her head and walked away.

Frankly, she should have pushed him into the ditch. True, we all bring along some bias from our native habitat, but to use it as a cultural filter is about as helpful as a stack of Bibles in a whorehouse. When heading to a new country, you have to leave your preconceived notions behind. Otherwise, why bother flying all the way to Europe—you can just tune in to the travel channel on cable TV and watch a bunch of tourists wearing berets and drinking wine at some faux Hemingway bar in EuroDisney.

Or perhaps that's not what the author means at all. He goes on to say that he is searching for the "macro in the micro," or the large truth in the small observation, and even if that is not possible, personal experience is still worth recording because it is all part of history.

Now, he's talking. So, let's observe.

AOÛT

Precisely on the first day of August, the weather system hanging over the Sahara decides to go north for a holiday, grabbing the jet stream across the Mediterranean and then taking a left turn for the Marais. That morning, we wake up to find the mercury has already sailed through the 30°C mark and is on its way to setting a record.

By the time I finish my breakfast coffee and head out for the morning shop, rue Barbette has already become a cauldron, with the sun reflecting off the façades of south-facing buildings and blasting into even the most remote slivers of shade. The ginger tomcat that normally sleeps on the ragtop Fiat in a courtyard off rue Vieille du Temple has taken refuge under the car, laying its belly across the cobbles in search of some feeble respite. The beggars stationed beside the cash machine on rue Pavée barely rattle their change cups, and the only lively street scene is in front of the Berthillon ice cream stand, where clerks are doing their valiant best to serve the long line of tourists in bulging Lands' End khaki shorts and neon running shoes.

As I leave Franprix with my groceries, I overhear a tourist couple in the midst of a meltdown. "Would you listen to me, for Chrissake! Notre-Dame is that way!" A man and a woman are standing near the Saint-Paul Metro station. She is leaning against a newspaper kiosk, her shoulders slumped under the weight of a knapsack. He is holding a map and pointing toward Minsk. I want nothing more than to sit in the shade and drink something very cold and alcoholic, like the six-pack of Kronenburg beer tucked under my arm. I succumb, however, to one of my more lamentable character traits and offer assistance.

"Are you lost?"

The husband doesn't even look up from his map. "Beat it."

"Have a nice day, asshole." How he was going to do that with a can of beer shoved sideways up his butt I didn't know, nor was I about to waste one to find out, but the thought alone was sufficient to cheer me up.

My reaction to the lost couple reveals to me an inner metamorphosis. Even though it has barely been a month since we arrived in Paris, I no longer feel like a tourist—almost without noticing it, I am starting to go native.

When I first arrived, for instance, I assumed a baguette was just an anorexic loaf of bread. These long, crusty cylinders serve as one leg in the stool of every French meal, the other two being coffee and cigarettes. Very soon, however, I realized that not all baguettes are created equal. Some are thin and flat, perfect for spreading with Dijon mustard and creating a ham and cheese sandwich; others are round and spongy, ideal for slicing into tiny *foie gras* platforms.

And some are so crusty you can bust your teeth. Since baseball is almost non-existent in France, I don't know what these are used for. Perhaps loan sharks favour them as a means of persuading recalcitrant debtors to pay up; I'd certainly hate to get cracked on the shins with one. After making the mistake of purchasing a broom handle from a pastry thief down the street, I go in search of a baguette source that is far less abusive to the molars. I discover a *boulangerie* near rue de Bretagne, where the Garcia family prepares strawberry tarts, chocolate cake, apple strudel, and hundreds and hundreds of baguettes, three times a day. "If you do not want a crusty baguette, you must ask for *pas trop cuit*," explains Madame Garcia, her face beaming. On behalf of my dentist, I thank her profusely.

I am also picking up on the more subtle rhythms and pulses of the neighbourhood. From where I sit in my living room, for instance, I can tell the location of the municipal garbage truck at any given moment by the sound of the car horns stuck behind it. If the level of noise approaches that of a 747 taking off at Charles de Gaulle Airport, then I know it is lumbering along rue Vieille du Temple. If the hubbub falls off precipitously, with only one or two little Citroëns peeping like chickadees, then it has turned onto rue Barbette.

I have also cottoned onto *Pariscope*, having seen hordes of locals consulting it while drinking their evening espresso. On Wednesday morning, I purchase the thick weekly guide for a few francs at the newsstand in front of the Hôtel de Ville. Sitting at home, I work my way through the thousands of cultural, theatre, and film events listed until I note a walking tour of the Marais that is leaving from the Saint-Paul Metro station within the hour. I immediately grab my camera and set out to learn a few nuggets about my new neighbourhood.

As I head down the circular stairs, my nose is assaulted by the antiseptic smell of *Monsieur Propre*. At the base of the stairs, Madame Greco is furiously scrubbing the ancient cobblestones with a broom. She shouts at me, but the noise outside on the street is deafening and I cannot make out a word. Perhaps she is saying good morning, or maybe she's giving me the rhubarb for tracking dog shit onto her pristine rocks. Not taking any chances, I cheerfully wave and sprint for the double doors.

The Marais has its own mini-version of a traffic jam whenever a *livraison*, or delivery, occurs. Residents' cars occupy all of the sites set aside for commercial parking by the municipality, so the delivery trucks must stop in the middle of the road. Owing to a lamentable lack of medieval foresight, the lanes are far too narrow to allow two Peugeots to pass side by side, and the installation of steel posts, or kingpins, in the curb at three-metre intervals precludes using the sidewalk as a convenient detour. Drivers stuck behind a truck must therefore occupy themselves until the deliveryman finishes his business.

A short distance down rue Barbette, a van has stopped to make a drop at the old-folks home, and the drivers caught behind are expressing their pleasure with a klaxon symphony. As I walk up the street, I notice that, after horn blowing, the most popular activity in a Paris traffic jam seems to be arm waving. Although every driver possesses a cellphone that is continually in use while the car is in motion, the moment he finds his car impeded, he puts his phone down, freeing both hands for communicating. The left hand is stuck out the window and waved, fingers pointed upward, while the heel of the palm of the right hand firmly applies pressure to the horn at the centre of the steering wheel. This is the only form of exercise I have ever seen a Parisian perform.

I arrive at the Saint-Paul Metro station and join about a dozen other people gathered in front of the main entrance. Janice, a small, rotund English woman in her early forties, is holding up a bright green umbrella, the knob of which is shaped like a frog. Once we have gathered round and paid our 60 francs, she begins to lecture in a voice guaranteed to carry over the din of a major French highway.

"Marais means marshland, and it was difficult to settle because the river Seine periodically flooded its banks. The Romans came in 52 BC and tried to make a town here, but it was too swampy, and they moved it to the Left Bank, where the Latin Quarter is today."

According to Janice, around the sixth century, a group of monks, seeking solitude, built the first settlement on the Right Bank. They assumed, quite reasonably, that a large expanse of mosquito-ridden mud might do the trick and weren't unduly pestered by neighbours for hundreds of years while the swampland slowly drained. Gradually, the Right Bank became more settled, until the need arose to incorporate it into the city proper.

Holding her green amphibian aloft, Janice leads her troupe down a narrow laneway until we come to a remnant of the Philippe Augustus wall. "This wall was ordered built by the king in 1190. He needed a fortified city while he went off to the Crusades." The wall, constructed of thick limestone blocks, was eight metres high and almost five kilometres long. Parisians universally revered the King for creating such a fine pile of stone and, as soon as he left for the Crusades, began to pull it down for their own renovation projects.

We cross rue Saint-Antoine and head north, toward the former site of the Hôtel des Tournelles. It was here that King Henri II, during a jousting tournament in 1559, was run through the eye with a lance by his Scots constable, Montgomery. He suffered in agony for ten days, until he finally died. Henri's wife, Catherine de Medici, was understandably upset and had the palace torn down.

Linda's boss, David, is especially interested in Henri II when I tell him all this a few days later. "You say he got stuck in the *eye* with a lance?" he exclaims. "Man, that's *gotta* hurt." David is a *chineur*, or bargain hunter. He asserts that haggling is in his blood, having been born in Lebanon and raised in Texas. Every weekend, for the last four years, he has taken his Range Rover to flea markets throughout the Paris region. By his own estimate, he has spent over $100,000 collecting silverware, grandfather clocks, and antique furniture, including several pieces from the reign of Henri II. It is, he readily admits, an addiction.

From what I can tell, approximately every second Parisian seems to have a similar proclivity. We are in the open-air Vanves flea market, located on avenue Georges Lafenestre in a quiet neighbourhood in the 14th arrondissement. About three hundred *brocanteurs* have piled their stalls high with everything from suede shoes to Limoges chinaware. Some specialize in watches or Louis XVI furniture, but most offer an eclectic cornucopia of junk that reminds me of the piles of useless old stuff my mother keeps in her basement. All of the stands are surrounded by thick crowds of bargain hunters, like magpies in a cornfield.

"The professionals arrive at 6:30 AM to pick over everything, looking for the good stuff," explains David. As we speak, Gérard, dressed in a wrinkled army jacket and exceedingly worn jeans, stops to say hello. David and Gérard greet warmly with a hug, and David asks if he has purchased anything. Gérard adopts a dismissive look, the corners of his lips curling down as his shoulders rise, to indicate that he was very foolish indeed to buy anything from these thieves. "One or two little things," he admits. We shake hands and continue on our separate ways.

Parisians take great pride in their appearance and rarely go out in public in anything less than immaculate attire. Once we are out of earshot, I comment on Gérard's old clothing.

"Everyone dresses like a pauper and pleads poverty when they come to the flea markets," explains David. "Wait until you see him at his shop in Saint-Ouen."

David stops at a stall operated by Paul, a dealer from north of Paris. Paul has a decidedly cadaverous look and is cradling a splinted finger. I wonder if it was broken over a disagreement about the provenance of his wares. We pick through a pile of kitchenware until David finds two silver-topped decanters listed at 100 francs each. He dickers with Paul, driving the price down by half.

As we slowly troll along, David explains the basic rules of flea markets. "Know your stuff, go early, never be afraid to walk away, and always negotiate." He taps his wallet, buttoned out of sight in his jacket. "Also, pay cash. I keep 10,000 francs in my pocket because cash price is always the best price."

David pauses at a stall run by a dealer with a face that a horse thief would admire and asks about what he has in the back of his truck. The man leads us into an old battered van and points to a sack containing pieces of carved wood, explaining that it is a genuine Louis XIV vanity. To my untrained eye, it looks like a bag of Louis XIV kindling, but the dealer wants 85,000 francs.

David whispers in my ear. "I think I can bargain him down to 60,000 francs." I drag him out of the van, back to fresh air and reality.

David forgets about the vanity the moment he spots a hand grenade sitting on a *brocanteur*'s table. "Is this real?" he asks, tapping it smartly on the wooden tabletop. The dealer distracts David with a *papier-mâché* crumb catcher from the nineteenth century. Painted with black enamel and traditional

Chinese figures, it is in perfect condition except for one corner that has been chewed off by a dog. Putting down the grenade, David picks up the crumb catcher and asks the dealer for a price.

The man offers it for 90 francs. "It is the price I would give to my mother," he whispers to me.

They dicker for a few moments, but the dealer doesn't budge. David eventually pays full price, happily carrying away his new possession. He points to a similar crumb catcher in better condition at another table. "Look what they want for this same thing— 1,200 francs!" I silently decide to give my mother a call and ask her to mail me her basement. I figure I could be a millionaire in two weeks.

August progresses like a blast furnace, with dire consequences. We are awakened early one morning by an explosion in our closet.

"What was that?" cries Linda.

I gingerly open the closet door to discover a heart-wrenching scene of destruction. *Crack!* Another bottle of champagne, one of six Piper-Heidsieck Bruts resting in a wine rack, bursts. I slam the door shut as shards of glass fly through the air, pinging off the sides of the closet. *Crack!* Like a string of moist firecrackers, each bottle auto-destructs until I am left with an expensive puddle of foamy syrup seeping from beneath the door.

Antoine, the champagne *caviste* on rue des Archives, is less than solicitous when I tell him my horror story. "What are you, some kind of idiot? You never store champagne at more than 20°C. The atmospheric pressure drops and *boum*, you could lose an eye."

Didier, Antoine's assistant, nods in agreement. "My uncle once had one explode and a shard sliced a hole in his throat." He does a rather grisly pantomime of the ensuing fountain of blood. "Thank God for the cork."

I cringe. There are a lot of qualities I admire in a wine, but the ability to perform tracheotomies is not one of them. Since I have no access to a nice, cool cellar, I decide to forgo any more champagne until the weather improves. I leave Antoine's establishment in search of an alternative.

Not that I had many places to search. August is the traditional holiday month in France, and most Parisians have taken advantage of their annual leave to escape Paris. All along the rue Vieille du Temple, the butcher, baker, and wine shops are closed. Even the novelty store that sells sequined handcuffs has been shuttered for the month. Talk about inconvenient.

Those who remain behind, like Jean-Pierre, the panhandler, are stoic about discharging their duties. Every morning, before the heat becomes intolerable, he positions himself by the Saint-Paul Metro station and diligently accumulates pocket change from commuters. He is perhaps seventy years old, with a face roughened by a scraggly white beard and a thick head of white hair tucked under a bright green baseball cap. Jean-Pierre is a happy man, proud of his profession, and greets everyone with a full set of crooked, stained teeth. For those who give him change, he has a special blessing, wishing them a safe journey and no *grèves*.

Jean-Pierre doesn't smell of cheap booze or soiled clothing; for all his dishevelment, he is quite clean. He is also quite popular with the ladies. On several occasions, I have noticed women stopping to chat and socialize, and they always give him a few affectionate kisses on the cheek before going on their way. Whatever the problem is that led him to beg on the streets, it isn't bad breath.

I stop and give Jean-Pierre a few francs, and comment on the heat in my bad French. "Where are you from?" he asks.

"Canada."

"Have a good day, eh?" he says in English, a big grin spreading across his face. He shakes my hand, and I notice his knuckles are stiff and swollen with arthritis. Suddenly, my champagne woes seem insignificant.

By now, I have noticed that Parisians love to take to the streets. Starting at about noon, the sidewalks begin to fill with older women wearing bright red lipstick and Chanel shoes, young couples pushing baby strollers, chain-smoking writers heading for their favourite cafés, and teenagers with cellphones surgically attached to their ears. The first French person to invent a package of cigarettes that you can dial will become a billionaire.

The long, warm evenings are especially perfect for socializing outdoors. The twentieth of August is the official church day for Saint-Bernard, so we decide to celebrate with a snifter of brandy at an outdoor café. It is a deceptively beautiful evening, with a cool breeze blowing across a crystal clear, cobalt blue night sky. When we reach rue Vieille du Temple, the cafés and bars are full of revellers in miniskirts, not all of them women. Above street level, the sounds of music and clinking glasses emanate from open windows. People wander arm-in-arm down the middle of the road, eating ice cream cones and flirting with passing strangers. Just as we cross the junction of rue Vieille du Temple and rue Sainte-Croix de la Bretonnerie, a thunderstorm comes rumbling up the river, gathering ferocity as it cuts north. A curtain of rain rushes down the street, knocking over the Moroccan fruit stand and sending everyone scrambling for cover. Within seconds, the sidewalk tables are deserted and everyone is huddling inside the bars until the rain abates.

Later that night, after the storm has passed, and the sky has cleared, Linda and I sit in our living room enjoying the cool breeze that wafts through the open windows. The streets have fallen silent, except for a man singing Italian arias. He is a magnificent tenor, and the notes carry along the long, narrow streets, echoing off the buildings. He turns a corner and continues on his way, but we can hear him long after he has passed, singing a lullaby to the city.

Toward the end of August, the heat wave finally begins to break, and I am startled by the whiff of cool air that clings to the shaded part of rue Barbette as I make my way east toward place Sainte-Catherine.

The square is a tiny space, perhaps fifty metres a side, and is crowded with sycamore trees and cafés. It is named after a convent that sat on the site in the thirteenth century, built at a time when Catherine was considered by poets and virgins to be one of the most helpful saints in heaven.

I like to collect stories about the weirder saints, which seems to exclude few. According to her hagiography, Catherine was an eighteen-year-old virgin living in Alexandria, at the mouth of the Nile. In those days, maidenhood was no barrier to evangelism, and she so persistently argued the Christian faith in the souks of the ancient capital that the apoplectic emperor finally had her beheaded, just to get some peace and quiet, I suspect. Her corpse immediately rose into the air and flew to Mount Sinai, her head presumably trailing like a faithful balloon. This was considered sufficiently miraculous to justify sainthood and, in the Middle Ages, a convent in the Marais was established in her name. Taking heed of Catherine's example, the women were prohibited from wagging their tongues, funnelling their energies instead into the avid cultivation of cucumbers.

The sky is a magnificent blue and I decide to do what any sane Parisian would do on such a day—linger over an espresso and read the morning newspaper. Whenever I come to a new city, I take time to go through the local rags. Befitting the modestly self-styled galactic headquarters for French culture, there are at least half a dozen daily papers in Paris, ranging from the scholarly *Le Monde* to the satirical *Canard enchaîné*.

Of all the local newspapers, I prefer *Le Parisien*. The tabloid is full of cops-and-robbers stories and tirades against the green mayor, but it also gives me what I want most, the invaluable information the average citizen needs to get through the day. *Le Monde* can tell me more than I want to know about the French state of mind regarding the impact of American hegemony (in the form of hamburgers sold by an orange-haired clown), but it won't warn me to watch out for the pickpockets working the Châtelet Metro station. *Le Figaro* can fill me in on the latest presidential pronouncements from the Palais Elysées (I am not a liar), but it won't help me pick the favoured horse in the fourth race at Le Hippodrome.

Le Parisien comes with a back page that alone is worth the 80 centimes. The top portion is the five-day meteorological forecast, in case you want to plan a *pique-nique* for Saturday. The bottom portion is a map of the city showing Metro closures, roadwork, and strikes. The union of exotic dancers is staging a march in Montmartre to expose the sordid state of their pension plans, and ten thousand angry motorcyclists are gathering at the Bastille to protest the law against driving on sidewalks. In addition, the Seine has flooded, and all the highways that rim its banks downtown are closed. Now, you tell me whether or not that's important information to live by.

Perhaps, I decide, a walk is in order. Finishing my espresso, I wander back to rue Vieille du Temple, stopping at the bakery for my *petit déjeuner*. A German couple wearing shoes more suited to traversing volcanic craters than Paris streets are trying to order muffins made with organic cereal. "*Sans préservatifs*," says the woman, inadvertently demanding that the hapless counter girl leave out the condoms. After they depart in frustration, I order a typical Parisian breakfast, *chausson aux pommes*, a buttery puff pastry filled with apple jam, and a diet Coke. Thus fortified with an excellent and hearty repast, I continue down to the river.

The pont Louis Philippe was built by the eponymous French monarch in 1865 to connect the Right Bank to Ile Saint-Louis. It replaced a decrepit old bridge that had been home to illicit jewellery shops and bordellos since the Middle Ages. It is now a wide, modern bridge that serves as a feeder for the busy highway that runs along the north shore of the Seine. Parisians haven't decided yet if this is an improvement. This morning, however, the voie Georges Pompidou, to give the highway its proper name, is blissfully deserted. True to the report in *Le Parisien*, the Seine runs swift and high, its brown, turgid water lapping over the stone banks and onto the asphalt, blithely converting the voie into a two-lane duck pond.

The Seine is the reason that Paris is here in the first place. The original settlers, the Parisii tribe, were a group of rather hapless Celts who eked out a living fishing mud carp off the bottom of the river. When the Romans arrived in 52 BC, however, they liked the site so much that they amiably dispatched the Parisii at sword-point and founded a colony. Over the years, the confluence of the Seine and the Marne proved its value as an economic crossroad, and the settlement flourished to the point where the kings of France established their royal court on Ile de la Cité. The Catholic Church, never one to miss a golden franchise location, constructed Notre-Dame across the street.

I look down into the water and spot what appears to be a yellow motorcycle helmet bobbing by. I wonder briefly if an angry motorcyclist is still attached by chinstrap to the helmet, his Vespa gripped between his thighs, protesting the law that forbids riding scooters in the Seine. As I ponder this image, several men in bright red wet suits emerge from beneath the bridge, in rather languid pursuit of the helmet. They are followed by a police boat from which a sergeant supervises with a bullhorn. I conclude I am witnessing either a rescue practice or the Parisian version of water polo.

I continue south to the pont Saint-Louis, a pedestrian bridge that leads to Notre-Dame Cathedral. At the end of the bridge, halfway down the steps leading to the quay, squats a man. He is about twenty years old, dressed in a black leather jacket and whistling to a flock of seagulls. Incredibly, several people have gathered to watch. I try to imagine what they are thinking. Here it is, a beautiful sunny morning in Paris and we are out on a stroll along the Seine. Should we stop to listen to the jazz busker playing "Basin Street Blues" on his tiny, portable piano? Or, how about watching the man riding a miniature bike in circles while juggling dinner plates? Forget all that—let's watch the bird caller.

I shouldn't be so cynical. The crowd is no doubt aware that this young man has spent several years at the "Ecole des Chansons des Oiseaux," honing his art at the feet of the masters, learning to gently coax these shy, retiring birds to his outstretched hand with nothing more than the seductive warbling of his voice, all to earn the adoration of an appreciative crowd. And no doubt he would have, too, if a six-year-old boy hadn't dumped his bag of stale popcorn onto the sidewalk. The gulls rise as one and swoop down upon this feast of manna, scattering the crowd and breaking the bird caller's heart.

Most people who visit Notre-Dame remember the striking west façade of the building, the twin, square towers soaring to the sky. From a very personal perspective, I find the back end of Notre-Dame far more interesting. A small park dedicated to Pope John XXIII marks the east side. The park, about the size of a large urban backyard, is exquisitely landscaped. The edge flanking the Seine has been planted with ivies, their immense trunks looping over the stone abutment and draping themselves above the river like a green, rustling curtain. At the centre, beneath the stony gaze of the Virgin Mary, a line of boxwood shrubs has been shaped into an intricate symmetrical pattern. Along the north side, two lines of chestnut trees have been tightly pruned to create a living arbour.

It is from this park that the flying buttresses, the immense external arches that support the walls of the cathedral, are visible in all their glory. They are like the exposed hoops of a grand dame's ball gown, or the ribs of some fantastic, extinct dinosaur. The bone-coloured sandstone buttresses spring from the ground and curve upward toward the cathedral, so graceful in form that when they touch upon the wall, it is with the softness of a kiss. If you are a fan of big buttresses, like I am, then this is heaven.

Leaving the park, I descend a narrow set of stone steps to a wide, cobblestone quay that runs along the south side of the river. It is closed to traffic and, thus, is much more charming, not to mention safer, for wandering than the traffic-choked quai de la Tournelle. Several barges are permanently docked along the water's edge, some with umbrellas and patio furniture on deck. They serve as full-time residences, complete with running water and electrical hookups. I imagine they must be quite damp and cold in the winter, as well as noisy; the old steel hulls bump against the stone docks whenever the wash of a tour boat sweeps against them.

A group of hoboes have set up permanent camp beneath the pont de la Tournelle. They have rummaged up some cots and blankets, and a large steel barrel in which they burn slats pulled from old wooden pallets. As I pass by, one man is carefully shaving himself over a wooden bucket, with a large, old-fashioned razor. His black Labrador retriever, wet from a recent swim in the river, watches him closely.

I am drawn farther east by the sight of a fishing derby being held on the quai Saint Bernard. The quay is the permanent home of the Musée de la Sculpture en Plein Air, which houses a collection of bizarre, abstract works, in various states of vandalism. My favourite is a bronze statue, its nameplate long since destroyed, of a man gleefully inserting his arm up what appears to be a large intestine. It reminds me of a farm veterinarian performing artificial insemination on a cow.

It turns out that the fishing derby is the national long-pole championship. All of the contestants have five-metre, fiberglass rods dangling sedately over the roiling waters, and several wear team jackets announcing official sponsorship deals. Like the original inhabitants of Paris, these men are hunting the elusive mud carp, not only for personal enjoyment, but for bragging rights, as well.

Hunger is definitely not a motivation. Paris has restaurants for every conceivable type of food, but a mud carp *brasserie* is one thing you will never see. Even French pigeons won't eat something that spends its days sucking on the bottom of the Seine. As I walk past the plastic barrels where the contestants store their catch, I wonder about the judging criteria. Do they have a prize for the fish with the most eyes? How about the highest lead content? Do they preserve the winning fish in formaldehyde and donate them to museums? The only institution that might want them, I suspect, is Ripley's Believe It or Not.

On the way back home, I pause at Albert Schweitzer Square, just off the quai des Célestins. The square is the former garden of the Duc d'Aumont, and his mansion still stands at the north end. Aumont is today remembered mostly for his amorous wife, who took advantage of his frequent absences to seduce clergymen. Parisians still laugh about the time the cardinal of Reims had to hide in a closet butt-ass naked when the Duke came home unexpectedly.

It's not the red of a cardinal's cloak that attracts me to the square, but a blanket of scarlet. A half dozen virginia creepers have been carefully trained to climb a stucco wall, creating a massive blanket of leaves that undulates in the breeze. Almost overnight, it has transubstantiated from deep emerald to brilliant ruby. It is so beautiful that it takes me a second to realize what it signifies—summer is over, and fall is just around the corner.

SEPTEMBRE

am attempting to study French irregular verbs in the living room when the sound of an angry mob fills rue Barbette. Several explosions rend the air, and the accompanying screams of terror are so shrill that my blood runs cold. Grateful for the distraction, I leap to the window, expecting to see a horde of pitchfork-waving vigilantes carrying some hapless aristocrat to the guillotine. To my disappointment, I am confronted instead by a crowd of teenagers clad in baggy jeans surrounding a pimply adolescent with a pocketful of firecrackers. School, I surmise, is in.

And, unfortunately, it is "in" in rue Barbette. Normally I am in favour of educating the young—I had to suffer through it, so why shouldn't they?—but I prefer it be done at a more civilized location. The French government owns spots that are sufficiently isolated for the installation of nuclear power plants and virus laboratories. Why not use them for high schools, as well?

Not only are the students in possession of explosives but, far worse, many of them are also equipped with *motards*. By official count, there are some 200,000 motor scooters in Paris and, by my estimate, 199,990 of them are driven by young male teenagers suffering from hormone surplus. *Motards* share two common traits; one, they never stop, and two, they are very noisy. Like sharks that must keep moving forward to breathe, only with greater lethality, *motards* must keep rolling forward or they will fall over sideways. If this means detouring onto the sidewalk when faced with a traffic jam, so be it. Restaurant waiters pull tables back when a Vespa comes barrelling along. It's pointless to shake your fist at them; the police hand out three thousand tickets a month to violators, but this is confetti to diehard motorcyclists. They view a traffic ticket the same way they view stoplights or baby strollers—an irritating imposition that must be dodged.

When it comes to cars, Parisian drivers demand the newest, shiniest models, but not, for some unfathomable reason, when it comes to scooters. It doesn't matter how old the machine is—some of them still run on coal oil—as long as it has two wheels and no muffler. And if, for some mysterious reason, it has been shipped from the factory with a muffler, then a hacksaw will fix that soon enough.

As the ringing of the 9 AM school bell approaches, one particular offender, recently returned from vacation in Pamplona, enters into a bullfight with a pavement-bound cohort. Wheeling back and forth along the street, he charges into a twirling basketball jersey. Before I can introduce some piano wire into the contest, the school principal runs out, grabs the miscreants by the collar, and hauls them into the courtyard. Unfortunately, the blood-curdling screams stop. I subsequently scan our lease, but alas, there is no clause for escape from lower forms of education.

I soon discover that September also marks the return of neighbours from their August holidays. I arise late one Saturday morning, happy to have had the opportunity to sleep in without the usual educational fracas outside our window. I am also nursing a persistent and annoying headache from either a brain tumour or a wine-tasting expedition the evening before. Scratching my nude posterior, I make my way to the kitchen and turn on the coffee maker. Without thinking, I open the curtains of the window overlooking the courtyard.

Most residents of the Marais take great amusement from staring into a neighbour's living room a few metres away and watching the goings-on. We don't. For the last two months, we have been blessed with what I was later to learn is a rarity in Paris—privacy. The apartment across the way has been empty, the windows closed, the curtains drawn.

Until this morning, that is. Today a man sits at a breakfast table not three metres away. He is in his early fifties, with a shock of white hair and a pair of black-rimmed eyeglasses pushed back on his bald dome. He glances up briefly from his newspaper and waves a piece of toast in my direction. I quickly pull the curtain shut. Is that the Maestro? If so, then I have just flashed my landlord. I wonder, is this considered improper behaviour in his native Italy?

I am still mildly worried when we set off to have our Saturday brunch. In the foyer, we bump into our neighbour Margaret as she is taking her dog Churchill for his morning constitutional on rue Barbette. I take the opportunity to describe the man sitting across the courtyard and ask who it might be.

"Ah, that's *Ramon*." Margaret drops her voice a notch. "He married the Maestro's first wife, you know." When it comes to talking about the French, the English have a special way of speaking volumes with their eyebrows, and Margaret's go up and down in sequence as she pronounces "wife," bracketing the offending noun with quotation marks. I am immediately curious about what kind of wife needs eyebrow brackets, but it is time for lunch, and as anyone who spends more than two days in France learns, there are certain priorities.

Although I have been informed that there is nothing as salubrious for a hangover as a raw egg in cognac, I prefer my own personal remedy—*un hamburger et des frites*. Although the average medical practitioner would rather have his Mercedes repossessed than prescribe said cure, I have it on good scientific authority that it not only ameliorates a queasy stomach, but also promotes the emission of endorphins in the brain. I read it on the internet, so there.

Finding a good burger and fries in Paris is next to impossible; the average native would rather admit to eating cat food on a cracker. We had been informed that, in good stead, however, a decent facsimile could be had at the Moosehead.

The Moose, located near the Odéon Metro station in the 6th arrondissement, is decorated in what I consider normal Canadian decor. The walls are adorned with hockey helmets and snowshoes, and a two-metre Mountie, carved from wood with a chainsaw, stands guard by the door. The bar is crowded with a mix of garrulous Australians, Brits, Canadians, and Yanks, kind of an English-speaking flotsam washed up on these Gallic shores. Cocktails on offer include the Maple Dew, a lethal mix of Canadian whiskey, maple syrup, and crème de menthe, and the Loose Moose, a seductive concoction of rum, cranberry juice, and orange juice. I highly recommend both to anyone seeking a good case of diabetes.

As promised, the menu features various kinds of burgers, including my favourite, a cardiologist's nightmare of bacon, cheese, and butter-fried mushrooms. We belly up to the bar and are greeted by Mark, the owner. When he learns that we are Canadian, he rolls up his shirtsleeve to show us a red maple leaf tattooed on his right arm and asks how long we are visiting. When I explain that we have been living in the Marais for the last three months, he pours us two large glasses of draft on the house and asks us what we think of Paris.

"We love it."

Mark laughs over his shoulder as he heads for the kitchen with our orders. "You must be friggin' nuts."

There is something about biting into a properly grilled burger that immediately transports me back home. For a moment, I am not in the middle of an immense city. Instead, I am sitting on a lakeside dock on a quiet summer evening, eating my supper and listening to the loons as they call across the still, translucent waters. Now that, I think, is a good burger. Friggin' nuts, indeed.

Although the burger cures my hangover, it does nothing to satisfy my curiosity regarding Ramon. Walking home from the bakery several days later, I spot my quarry trying to negotiate a large old bicycle into our foyer. I hold the door and invite my mysterious neighbour up for a coffee and croissant.

It turns out that Ramon is an international fashion photographer based in the Burgundy region of France. A long-time Paris resident, he has lived in the Marais, on-and-off, for the last two decades, and often stays in the Maestro's apartment while travelling through Paris on assignment.

Ramon's personal history is intimately tied to that of our apartment. In the early 1980s he met Isabella, who had recently separated from the Maestro, taking their young son Pascal with her. The Maestro, who lived on a barge outside the city, wanted to see more of his boy after the separation and offered to buy a space and convert it into two apartments, so that they could live side by side. Ramon, Isabella, Pascal, and the Maestro thus ended up as one big happy household in the Marais. Now, I ask you, could there by a happier French ending?

I have one more question: what's with the ugly duck in the dining room? According to Ramon, it is, in fact, a cormorant. The picture was much beloved by all concerned and had been mounted in a prominent spot to display their affection for the motley avian.

"I don't care—that bird's gotta go," Linda announces, when I tell her Ramon's explanation later that evening. "It leers at us whenever we cook fish."

Agreed. But a blank wall is just about as unappetizing as the current rendering of a muddy-toed fish-muncher. What to put in its place? The Sopwith Camel propeller, while suitably rakish, would require something along the lines of a fifteen-centimetre steel bolt to hold it in place. Other pieces of art, including a rather pleasing, surrealistic rendition of the Andes, are already holding down places of honour in the living room. The only solution is to get something new.

Fortunately, we are in the right place. More than one visitor to the Marais has observed that a dog can't piss in this neighbourhood without hitting an art shop. Every block has at least one, sometimes as many as three. They sell everything from oil paintings to bronze sculpture, for every conceivable taste. There are studies of nuns eviscerating Christ, brightly-lacquered silhouettes of cows cut from thick steel, female torsos shaped from latchkeys, hedgehogs blown from glass, and immense mosaics sculpted from the bottom of plastic pop bottles.

We drop into an open house at a *galerie* on rue Vieille du

Temple to view an avant-garde display. The gallery is featuring the works of a Parisian painter who evidently draws her inspiration from Hieronymus Bosch and R. Crumb in equal measures. Her tableaux feature male and female figures disembowelling each other while household pets observe approvingly. According to her promotional literature, the *artiste* is motivated by an extreme honesty, breaking taboos and allowing the sexuality repressed within the subconscious to be revealed. I am not certain how this relates to the portrait of a woman making sandwiches from slices of her own thigh, but Linda likes the way she draws cats. Finding the overlying food metaphor not to our taste, however, we decide to keep searching. Following the advice of Ramon, we visit the place des Vosges.

The *place* has a fascinating history. It is the original site of the Hôtel des Tournelles, a royal residence until Henri II's eye-poking incident and it was torn down. In 1610, Henri IV used the empty space to construct one of the most sumptuous condo projects in the world.

Now known as the place des Vosges, the square consisted of thirty-six symmetrical houses positioned around a large space shaded with chestnut trees. As in Aspen, Colorado, everyone who was anyone had a house there. Those too far down the A-list were relegated to building on the fringes, so minor royalty and government ministers bought up their own pieces of swamp and began piling stones. The nearby Hôtel Salé, built in 1656 by the king's salt tax collector, now houses Picasso's personal collection of art. The Hôtel de Rohan, built for the Bishop of Strasbourg to live in when he wasn't praying or chasing married women, is so immense that the national archives currently stores its entire collection of six billion documents there.

The end of the place des Vosges's heyday came in 1682,

when Louis XIV decamped to Versailles. The nobility faithfully followed, and by the end of the nineteenth century, most of the square and surrounding Marais had been converted into tenements, factories, and workshops.

And that would have been that, had it not been for the intervention of President Charles de Gaulle in 1962, who pronounced the Marais a national treasure worth saving. A flood of public money restored the old mansions, and a wave of gay designers opened chic fashion shops and cafés, driving rents through the roof.

For some reason that escapes me, the place des Vosges has become the home to "mixed-media" art. We visit the *atelier* of a prominent mix-master who weaves male and female torsos in steel wire. When a spotlight shines through the torso, it projects a three-dimensional shadow onto the wall behind. The moment I see his work, however, I am filled with an intense desire to perform X-rated shadow-puppet shows, and the gallery owner hustles us unceremoniously out the door. Turns out, everybody's a critic.

We are about to give up our search when something catches Linda's eye. There, in the window of Galerie des Medicis, is our painting. It depicts, in broad pallet knife strokes of brightly-coloured oil, a rural scene from the Provence countryside. The foreground is a black olive grove, the scrub beneath its branches burnt to a brilliant rusty orange. In the distance, the white limestone peaks of the Luberon loom over the landscape, separating the aubergine sky from the earth below. The colours are bold, the composition is brilliant, and the perspective is breathtaking. We have to have it.

As it turns out, the gallery is holding an open house to honour the artist. We enter and are greeted by the assistant manager, a young woman who wears a black dress cut low enough to reveal a tan-in-a-can all the way to her navel. After being handed a glass of champagne and a brochure, we soon learn that the man-of-the-hour is Francis Riehl, an Alsatian-born artist now residing in Provence. Helpfully, the brochure contains a critique of Riehl's work that has been translated into English.

"Francis Riehl in all his work proclaims his desire to be directly inspired by the nature. To translate the brightness from it, he makes use of frank colours and is not afraid of setting them the some to the others."

Oddly enough, this is beginning to make sense, especially after my second glass of champagne.

"His concern is to achieve the strongest expression to translate the vitality of the earth and its plants blooming. The supernatural and the reality join then in a brilliance which returns vibrating surfaces and contains the light of an intense poetry."

With much trepidation, and not a little curiosity, we seek out the artist. Riehl, it turns out, vibrates much less intensely than expected, and is, in fact, a rather stress-free individual in a fleece vest. He has just returned from New York where his work has been received with great acclaim. We praise his skill and have a few more glasses of champagne, which eventually makes his works vibrate as promised. By the end of the evening, we have purchased a landscape, *Les Rochers Blancs*, for more than we can afford, but for far less than what it is worth. The next day, Richard, the gallery owner, delivers it to us personally, and we gleefully put the cormorant in the closet to make room for our masterpiece.

That night's salmon dinner, cooked *à la Provençal*, is absolutely delicious.

Rue des Rosiers lies about two blocks south of our home. The Jewish neighbourhood surrounding this narrow, crooked lane is old, even by Marais standards. The street was named for the rose bushes that grew at the base of the Philippe Augustus wall in the twelfth century. Working people, including bakers and milliners, made the street their home. The original houses, some of which survive today, were built with sandstone blocks and oak beams.

I enjoy walking along the *rue* whenever business or whim takes me in that direction. The eastern end of the lane begins at rue Malher. As you move west, the street narrows near Jo Goldenberg's restaurant. Although the Jews were among the first occupants of rue des Rosiers, they didn't start arriving en masse until the late nineteenth century, when religious pogroms in Poland and Russia drove them into exile. The Marais, at that time a run-down ghetto of tenements, provided cheap accommodation for the refugees. Several synagogues were built to accommodate their religion, and kosher bakeries and delis, like Goldenberg's, sprang up to service their material needs.

Thanks to the relatively benign attitude of French authorities, the Jews lived in peace until the Second World War, when the Germans invaded France. Under the Nazi thumb, the collaborationist government passed laws against Jews and began deporting them to concentration camps. Over the course of the war, more than two thousand adults and five hundred children were shipped from Paris to Auschwitz, where most of them perished.

But the remaining Jews didn't give up. Many of them joined the resistance, destroying the railways that connected Paris to the concentration camps and harassing the occupying army. When the Allies finally advanced toward Paris in August

1944, the people of the Marais rose in revolt with the rest of the city, seizing the Hôtel de Ville and setting up barricades along the major thoroughfares. For seven days, the resistance throughout Paris fought Panzer tanks with Molotov cocktails and handguns, until General LeClerc's army arrived. Much of the Marais was damaged, including the fifteenth-century Hôtel Hérouet, when the retreating Germans fired a barrage of artillery shells back into the city.

Most of the Goldenberg family died in Auschwitz, but young Jo came back to Paris after the Second World War to reopen the deli, which features a wide selection of treats, including pastrami on bagels and fat dill pickles. I stop in and buy a pastrami on bagel, which, frankly, is as dry as a cotton tea towel, but I am fascinated by a newspaper story that has been taped to the window beside a bullet hole. On the afternoon of 9 August 1982, while the restaurant was packed with lunchtime clients, four men got out of a car and threw a hand grenade into the dining room, then entered it, and began firing automatic weapons at the clientele, killing six and injuring twenty-two. Next, they strolled back down the street, firing at random. Although various suspects involved in the Palestinian movement were identified, no one was ever arrested.

Past Goldenberg's, the street zigzags along for several blocks, past bookstores, jewellery shops, and butchers. An old man sitting on the sidewalk sells the city's Hebrew newspaper, and fat women beg coins from people waiting in line to buy a falafel at one of the many takeaway shops. Near the west end of rue des Rosiers is a primary school, built in 1844. It is a sturdy, two-storey building with an enclosed yard filled with shouting children. On the façade of the school are two bronze, life-size bullheads, reminders that a meat market once occupied this site. A marble plaque also adorns the façade, bearing the inscription: "165 Jewish children were deported from this school and exterminated in the Nazi camps. Don't forget."

It is 11 September, mid-afternoon. I am sitting at my desk in the living room, contemplating the note I have made regarding the words on the plaque, when Linda calls from work and tells me to turn on the TV. Apparently, a plane has crashed into a building in downtown New York. I switch on TFI, one of the main French stations. The announcer is sitting at his news desk, a look of stunned disbelief on his face. The picture cuts live to New York on a clear, sunny morning. Media helicopters circle the World Trade Center, which is emitting a huge billowing mass of black smoke. From what I can understand of the voiceover, an airline jet has smashed into the building, causing unknown casualties. How could such an incredible accident occur? As I watch in horror, another plane appears and strikes the second tower. By the end of the day, America is at war with an unseen adversary.

As the intent of the enemy unfolds, it soon becomes apparent that no country is safe. A few days later, in Paris, French security forces arrest a group of terrorists who had been planning to blow up the American Embassy with a suicide car bomb. When I read about the plot, for reasons I cannot explain, I have to go and see.

Place de la Concorde is one of the prettiest spots in Paris. Bounded on one side by the Tuileries gardens, it is the eastern terminus of the avenue des Champs-Elysées, the broad and leafy boulevard that knits together many of the grandest monuments in the city. The place itself is a huge traffic circle, centred around the Obelisk, a 3,200-year-old Egyptian stone monument from Luxor.

The American Embassy sits at the northwest edge of place de la Concorde. Designed in the style of Haussmann's nineteenth-century vision, it is a massive pile of honey-coloured stone with an imposing entrance draped by the Stars & Stripes. Although traffic still moves through Concorde, the entire embassy has been blocked off by a circle of blue and white armoured personnel carriers of the French National police, and a black and yellow steel barrier has been erected across the gate that leads to the front entrance. Men in heavy body armour tote submachine guns as they stand guard, grimly confronting anyone who approaches too close.

It is a sad and depressing sight, and I decide to take the Metro back home. During the ride, I notice contrasting reactions to the terrorist attacks. There is a postman sitting beside me reading an article in a tabloid newspaper. I glance over his shoulder. It is a feature story on the nerve gas attacks carried out some years ago by a Japanese extremist group on a Tokyo subway. We pull into the Louvre station, and a man in a turban gets on carrying a paper bag. I look to my left. A Dutch woman in a black leather coat is staring at the man. A family of day trippers from Alsace cower against the far wall, trying to avoid contact. It's as though bin Laden himself got on the train. In contrast, the postman reading the newspaper glances up briefly at the new passenger, then calmly goes back to reading about mayhem.

I get out at the Saint-Paul Metro station, thankful to be alive. I am walking up the steps, when a familiar voice makes me turn. "Hey, Canada!" Jean-Pierre is standing at a wastebasket, digging through the debris.

"What are you doing?"

Jean-Pierre gives me a big grin. "Preparing lunch." He pulls a half-eaten falafel out of the garbage, delicately picks away a few cling-ons, then takes a bite. "A little too much cumin, but not bad." He holds it out to me. "Care for some?"

"No thanks. I don't have any appetite."

Jean-Pierre takes a white linen hankie from his pocket and delicately wipes some hummus off his lips. "What is wrong? You are ill, no?"

"No, it's the attack." I look around the tiny square, so close to the Jewish quarter, and wonder if it isn't time to schedule that much needed spine transplant. "What if they come here?"

Jean-Pierre shrugs and returns his attention to his meal. "One cannot worry about something that may never happen, *mon ami*."

Boy, these Parisians are a tough bunch. I give the panhandler a few coins, then make my way down to the Seine and Ile Saint-Louis. The calm, quiet neighbourhood, with its solid, square buildings, gives me comfort. I come to the pont de la Tournelle, which connects Ile Saint-Louis with the Left Bank. As I cross, I spot Notre-Dame to the west. An artist is standing before his easel, painting the façade. I am struck by the recollection of something I had read in the newspaper. Several Islamic extremists had been arrested in Strasbourg the year before while planning to blow up the city's cathedral, one of the most beautiful Gothic buildings in the world. What if some other group was plotting the same fate for Notre-Dame at this very moment? I turn and briefly scan the skies above the river valley.

I walk back along the Left Bank and cross over the pont de l'Archevêché, which also serves as Monique's open-air studio. The native Parisian is in her sixties and wears a dirty brown coat and a pair of woollen gloves from which she has cut the fingers, the better to hold her brushes and smoke her hand-rolled cigarettes.

I stop to look through Monique's portfolio. She has the usual watercolours of Notre-Dame and place des Vosges, but she has leavened the tourist fodder with the fronts of tiny hair salons and still-life studies of the pastries in bakery windows. There are even portraits of *bouquinistes*, the men selling books from green tin boxes that line the quai de Montebello.

In fact, Monique's subjects are everything that gives this city its charm. I decide to buy an architectural study of a nearby bistro. Monique is happy; it is her first sale of the day. With great dexterity, she flicks the stub of her cigarette off the bridge at an empty tour boat passing below. "The tourists, they have all gone home."

I nod. "They're afraid."

"Afraid? Afraid of what?" Monique starts to laugh, but a cough cuts her off, and only another cigarette can calm her lungs. When she finally gets her breath back, she tells me a story. "When we were children, the Nazis came. We hid in the forest of Vincennes and ate chestnuts."

I suddenly begin to suspect how fatalistic Parisians can truly be. After two millennia of invasions, civil wars, religious conflict, siege, starvation, and floods, there's not much that can make them sit up and take notice. "What, suicidal fanatics and a plane full of fuel? Please, I'm having my espresso."

I follow the road along the north side of the cathedral to the front façade. The normal waiting line of several hundred German and Asian tourists is absent, and I decide to go in. Passing from the bright sunshine into the interior gloom, I am immediately transported back several centuries in time. The din of the buses and cars diminishes to a whisper, and the solemn weight of medieval life settles upon my shoulders. The two lines of stone pillars flanking the centre of the church soar into the enclosed space, supporting the ceiling forty-five metres above. From aloft, light streams through arched windows, the rays of sun softened by the still, dusty air as they penetrate to the marble floor below. From above, the giant bell in the south tower begins to toll.

I move along the side aisle, stopping briefly to light a votive candle and admire the paintings in a tiny alcove. I continue on to the transept, where I have an excellent view of the rose windows—immense, stained-glass works of art that depict Christ, the saints, and the apostles. I notice there are several dozen people kneeling in the pews and praying, more than usual for a weekday afternoon. I recognize a woman who sells flowers on rue de Rivoli and a clerk from the dry cleaners. Perhaps not all Parisians are so cynical.

Just past the transept is the entrance to the treasury. The building is attached to the south side of the cathedral by a narrow, guarded hallway. Inside the treasury rests a collection of gilded reliquaries containing remnants of the saints, including the true crown of thorns worn by Christ.

Odd tales tend to cling to me like dust bunnies to a feather mop, and the story of how the crown came to rest in Notre-Dame is no exception. It seems that the wreath, placed on Christ's head by the Romans to mock his claim as "King of the Jews," was mysteriously spirited away from Jerusalem and ended up in the keeping of the emperors of Constantinople. During the Byzantine wars in the thirteenth century, the Emperor Baudouin, in need of funds, hocked the sacred relic to the Venetians. When he couldn't honour his pledge, the Venetians sold it to the French King Louis IX for an astronomical sum.

Louis took the relic back to Paris and had the Sainte-Chapelle constructed to house it. Over the years, the thorns were plucked from the crown and given to various heads-of-state at official banquets as souvenirs, or perhaps as toothpicks. The remains are now kept in the Notre-Dame Treasury, and trotted out each Easter on Good Friday to display before the devout. I think about this as I gaze around the cathedral. I say a brief prayer, hoping, knowing that Notre-Dame—and Paris—would survive.

OCTOBRE

By the beginning of October, the cylindrical metal garbage cans that dot every corner of the city have been replaced by translucent green plastic bags with *Vigipirate!* scrawled across the front, no doubt to encourage mad bombers into safely discarding any unwanted explosives. Paratroopers in black berets and semi-automatic rifles lounge stylishly in the Metro stations. A portable canteen on rue des Rosiers has been set up to serve *boeuf bourgignon* to the platoons of federal police that patrol the Jewish quarter. Parisians, it seems, have already adapted to the terrorist threat. I take my shopping cart and try to do the same.

As I cross rue des Archives in search of courgettes, the smell of freshly ground coffee grips me firmly by the nose. I jerk to a stop, peer through the window at a huge pile of burlap bags from Brazil, and surmise that this is the source of the olfactory adhesive. I enter. The tiny shop is dominated by an immense, stainless-steel coffee roaster. A very tall man, with wisps of hair sprouting randomly from his scalp, is bent over the roaster, stirring the beans with rapt attention.

I stand for several moments being categorically ignored. Finally, I cough. The coffee man rotates his head around like an owl and stares at me. "What do you want?"

Like a good Canadian, I stifle a wisecrack and stick to the

script. "I'd like to buy some coffee, please."

"What kind of machine do you have?"

"A flat-bottomed drip filter."

The coffee man shrugs as though my machine isn't fit for straining pigeon droppings, but he momentarily abandons his ministrations to lift down a package of beans marked *Spécial Fort* and grinds them to specification. "Anything else?"

Linda and I both enjoy the thick, heady taste of espresso in the morning, so I pick up a pack sitting on the counter. "I'd like some of this espresso."

"Do you own an espresso machine?"

"No, I'll just run it through my drip machine."

The coffee man reaches over the counter and snatches the bag out of my hand. "Espresso is for *espresso* machines." He sticks the bag out of sight and reach.

You don't argue with a man who keeps a hot roaster behind the till. I take my *Spécial Fort* home, brew it up, and find it to be surprisingly good. I can't help but imagine how nice the espresso would taste, however. I return the next week, again asking for some espresso.

The coffee man shakes his head. "You said you don't own an espresso machine."

I fall back on my innate knack for improvisation. "Um, I just bought one."

"Oh?" The coffee man arches one eyebrow. "What kind—the Ducatti 750 with dual injectors?"

"Yes, that's the one."

The coffee man smiles in triumph. "And how do you brew coffee with a *motorcycle*, Monsieur?"

Busted. I take my *Spécial Fort* and flee Inspector Poirot's lair.

To say that Paris retailing is a little different from the rest of the world's is a little like saying that Madonna has a minor ego issue. I am quickly learning that most French stores appear to exist in the same orbit as Pluto. One of the first lessons I discover in the Marais is that the hours that a shop is open bear no resemblance to common sense. The only method to their madness seems to be the coordination of closing times with maximum customer demand. As a typical example, the sandwich shop around the corner closes between noon and 2 PM. I assume the rationale is that it keeps overhead costs, like bread and tuna, to a minimum.

In addition, some grocery stores are open Sunday but closed Monday. All shops are open on Saturday, but wine stores, fish markets, and horse butcher shops close between 1:30 and 3:30 PM to conscientiously eliminate the potential threat to housewives of missing the afternoon soap operas. Most stores close by 6 PM, regardless of the day, because to stay open longer would deprive workers of the chance to consume their evening pastis before heading home, and the government doesn't want people rioting in the streets. At least not sober ones.

Each food store has its unwritten code of conduct, and woe to those who transgress it. There are two types of greengrocers, for instance: the point-and-pay variety, who doesn't allow the customer to personally choose and bag anything, but stands piously behind the wares picking what he thinks you should eat, and what I call the touchy-feely, who allows customers to wander the aisles and fondle at will.

We discover the distinction by accident. Stopping at a colourful display of pumpkins and squash one Saturday morning, we spontaneously decide to purchase some ingredients for the evening's meal. Linda, in her exuberance, marches in behind the narrow stall that fronts the store and begins rummaging around in a large wicker basket behind the counter.

The clerk has a look on his face not unlike that of an actor who, during the drawing room scene, discovers that one of the audience has mounted the stage and gone to the sideboard to pour a drink from the prop decanter. Horrified at the thought that this pretty woman might suddenly begin ransacking his till or, even worse, picking all the best fresh basil for herself, he begins to flap his hands behind her in a vain attempt to stir up enough breeze to blow her back to the sidewalk.

Linda, completely oblivious to his pantomime, continues to explore through his sanctum, examining the exotic mix of mushrooms that happens to be in season this week. Finally, much to his evident relief, she returns to the weigh scale, and he is able to reclaim his proper spot before the planet begins to tilt dangerously on its axis.

My theory is that the idiosyncratic nature of retailing is directly related to the needs of the *gourmet*, or French lover of food. Everyone, from Tuktoyuktans to Tasmanians, loves to eat, but the French *live* to eat. Paris has, by my estimate, four times more restaurants per capita than London has, and each one is full as soon as it opens its doors. An endless succession of lamb chops roasted in garlic, rump steak in Roquefort sauce, and green beans with chopped *foie gras* streams from tiny basement kitchens to the delight of the clientele. And dessert is not just the final course, it is a labial affair with a spoon. *Tartes framboises* of indescribable subtlety, concoctions of ice-cream-filled cake smothered in chocolate sauce, creamy custards of transcendental texture—all must be wickedly fondled with the tongue before being ingested.

Scientists have calculated that, in the course of their daily ministrations, the French suck back enough fat and cholesterol to give a rhinoceros a spare tire. So why don't they get fat? Medical researchers say that French slimness has something to do with red wine consumption, but I know the real truth. Thanks to their stores, the French spend half their entire adult lives shopping for groceries.

We have a bar fridge in our kitchen. Everyone in North America knows that a bar fridge is designed to hold twenty-four cans of beer and one can of tomato juice. That's the law. For some reason or other, the French don't get it. Not only are you expected to keep your beer in this fridge, but also pork chops, yoghurt, cucumbers, and frog's legs. What this means is that, in order to eat, you must go shopping every day.

Another wondrous feature of French shopping is the edict that prohibits one artisan from muscling in on another's turf. Thus, the butcher cannot sell cheese, the cheese merchant cannot sell bread, and the baker, font of all things pastry, risks humiliation in the public stocks if he ever so much as whispers *la saucisse* within the confines of his emporium.

As a result, to assemble the ingredients for a meal you have to hike more miles than Saint Paul did spreading the gospel. To make a simple curry, for instance, I must first go to the butcher on rue de Bretagne for the best lamb, then back across the river to little Vietnam in the 5th arrondissement for the freshest coriander and ginger, then finally to Israel's Epicerie du Monde on rue François Miron for ground cumin. No wonder the average Frenchman can suck back a six-course meal and then kick a soccer ball over the Eiffel Tower.

It is a mild fall day, the kind of day when the weak sun hangs low on the horizon, and the cold trees along the banks of the Seine give off a nascent mouldy smell, a harbinger of the advancing season. I am on my way to meet Linda for lunch in La Défense. I pick up a copy of *Le Parisien* from the press kiosk and hand Jean-Pierre the change from my purchase. Seeing the newspaper, he asks to have a look. Intrigued, I hand it over. Is he interested in the weather report? Or, far less likely, the help-wanted ads?

"I want to check the horses," he explains.

"You gamble on the horses?"

I suddenly want to ask him to return my change.

Jean-Pierre shrugs, an apologetic smile on his lips. "It is in my nature." Flipping to the sports section, he scans the racing sheet. "Ah, it is too bad—she is not running today."

"Who?"

"*Comble du Bonheur.*"

Odd name for a horse, that. I try to decipher the phrase in my head, but "the peak of good times" just doesn't sound right. I decide to ask Jean-Pierre the meaning.

The panhandler thinks for a moment. "Don't you ever stop and turn and look back from where you came, just in the hope of seeing someone smiling at you?"

"No."

Jean-Pierre twirls his fingers in a delicate arch. "Don't you ever pause to savour the way the baker decorates his éclairs with the tiny lines of white chocolate?"

"Sorry."

Jean-Pierre sighs. "Don't you even bet on the horses?"

"Can't say as I do."

Jean-Pierre hands me back *Le Parisien*. "Then, Canada, I cannot explain."

When I reach La Défense, Linda and Jim are waiting for me at the entrance to their office. Jim, a well-dressed bachelor from Winnipeg, has just been transferred from Jakarta to Paris to work with Linda's team. We walk down the main promenade to a patio overlooking the Grand Arch, the modern, marble-covered monument that apes the classic lines of Napoleon's triumphant monument in place d'Etoile. I start to regale them with shopping woes, but Jim dismisses my complaints with a wave of his hand. "You should just go to a *supermarché*—it has everything there. The French invented the supermarket you know—it's a fact."

If they invented the supermarket, they did it on laughing gas. We once lived on the Cook Islands in the middle of the Pacific Ocean, where, once a month, the supply ship would drop anchor and disgorge its contents. Overnight, the shelves of the central supermarket would be crammed with items that had long since disappeared—tinned fish, tomato sauce, and flour—and the entire island partook in an orgy of sardine pizzas.

In many ways, the Marais Franprix is our own personal Cook Island. One week, they are totally bereft of two-ply toilet tissue; the next, bright pink rolls of fluffy paper overflow into the aisles. Zip-lock bags, those indispensable icons of North American life, vanish with no warning, reducing us to quivering wrecks when we have to decide what to do with the leftover *foie gras*. The worst part is the niggling suspicion that they are not really out of zip-lock bags or two-ply toilet paper at all, just that they have moved them, for their own unfathomable reasons, to another section entirely.

Having been born in an Anglo-Saxon country, I make the normal assumption that toilet paper can be found with other paper household products, such as napkins and kitchen towels. But one can never, under any circumstances, rest comfortably with the Gallic logic that governs product placement. A French shelf stocker may look at the bright pink colour and decide, *naturellement*, that the toilet paper belongs with all the other bright pink products. The TP thus ends up with the Pepto Bismol, women's lingerie, and homeboy head scarves. This may be convenient to a female hoodlum suffering indigestion, but the average foreigner is left scratching his head in bafflement, which may be part of the motivation for doing it that way in the first place. I suspect there's nothing funnier to a pimply shelf jockey than the sight of a German shopper staggering up and down the aisles in a futile search for suppositories when they're sitting there right beside the gumdrops. They're heinous, this lot.

I am vainly contemplating similar mysteries of cultural nuance when someone knocks on our front door. I open it to discover a man of around fifty-five standing on our landing. He is dressed in a blue cardigan that is so old I wouldn't use it for moth bait, and his glasses sit slightly askew on a large bulbous nose. "Hello," he announces, in a vaguely Mediterranean accent tinged with embarrassment. "Where is my bird?"

He is speaking to me in English, but somehow, that doesn't seem to be of any particular help. "Did you say your bird?"

"Yes." He points down the hallway. "It was hanging in the dining room."

Suddenly this Daliesque conversation begins to make sense. The man at the doorway is the Maestro, my landlord. I hastily invite him in for a cup of coffee.

Making himself comfortable on a kitchen barstool, the Maestro explains that he is on a brief stay in Paris and, since the dining room wall is visible from his apartment across the courtyard, he noted the cormorant's absence. "It is special to me, and I want to find out where it has gone."

What could be so special about this bird, I wonder? Did he rescue it from the net of a swarthy Sicilian fisherman? I rather sheepishly explain that we had moved it to a safer exhibition spot, the back of our closet, to be precise.

"Ah!" The Maestro accepts this slight to his taste with elegant grace. "If you do not want it, I shall gladly hang it in my apartment."

Happy to have it off my hands, I go to the closet and open the door. The Maestro, peering over my shoulder, is puzzled. "You do not use the safe?"

"What safe?"

"The one behind the cormorant."

Sure enough, when we lift the canvas out, there is a small steel door, complete with tumbler, mounted in the cement wall in the back of the closet. "I didn't even realize it was there."

The Maestro pats the steel door. "It is a very good safe. The thieves could not break it open."

I have to admit, this makes me feel less good than intended. "Thieves?"

"Ah, yes." The Maestro squints his eyes at the memory. "They broke in through a courtyard window and ransacked both apartments. Here, I will show you the damage they left behind." Taking me into the living room, he stands before the double doors leading to his apartment. "I made these doors with my own hands, and look what they do." He points to several broken sections of wood. "There was nothing to steal, so they make a mess instead."

I stare at the broken jamb, vaguely worried. You can do

nastier things with a crowbar than chip wood. "Do you think they'll come back?"

The Maestro shakes his head. "No, they only come around when the home is empty—that is why I am glad you are here." He claps me on the back as he heads for the doorway. "Even if you do put my poor cormorant in the closet."

The second Sunday in October is Canadian Thanksgiving, and Jim invites us over for dinner. After packing the traditional French dinner gifts of a bottle of champagne and chocolate-dipped maraschino cherries into my backpack, we head across town on the #9 Metro line.

The #9 wanders through several Paris arrondissements, including the swank district around the presidential palace. But it also democratically serves some of the least desirable neighbourhoods in the city, and whether by purpose or neglect, takes its cue from the latter. The seats sport a grey, greasy layer of indeterminate composition, and the walls are covered with juvenile scrawls. It rattles along at slow speeds, swinging from side to side like a drunken python, the smell of disinfectant fighting a losing battle with decades of accumulated grime.

Regardless, the regular passengers on #9 obviously show a keen interest in national affairs. The attention of the woman sitting across from us is raptly focused on a tabloid widely available in most supermarkets. Reading the back page, I note that a prominent politician has been photographed leaving the residence of another man's wife in the early morning hours. According to a statement issued by his office, he had been conducting a personal poll. The results of his survey, no doubt, are expected to emerge within nine months.

Jim's home is located in the Trocadéro district, across the

river from the Eiffel Tower. The neighbourhood is markedly upscale from the Marais, with wide streets, modern buildings, and the distinct aroma of old money. Most notably, nobody walks along the ample sidewalks except the domestic help.

Jim's building is a modern, brick-covered edifice that stands beside its neighbours with a squat, looming presence. The foyer is adorned with Italian green marble and gilded wall fixtures, and the stairwell is a grand, spiralling affair with walnut panelling and red carpet. I imagine Mussolini would have felt quite at home here.

In contrast to the exterior, Jim's apartment has a warm, friendly ambience. Exploiting a natural talent for decorating, he has highlighted his teak furnishings with swaths of bright silk and Balinese prints, which he had brought, along with his friend Heri, from Indonesia.

By the time we arrive, the other guests are already congregating around the drink buffet. Pam, who is expecting her third child, is drinking Perrier. Her husband David is sampling champagne from Epernay. Giorgio, who hates bubbly, is wrestling the cork out of a Saint-Emilion red to pour for his wife, Sue.

Jim and Heri are busy cooking in the kitchen. The turkey, a nine-kilogram monster, has almost finished roasting in the oven, and the pair are fussing over various pots of mashed potatoes and squash, putting the final touches on the meal.

As soon as the turkey is done, Jim ushers everyone into the dining room. I look around the table. Jim, Linda, and I are from Canada, Heri from Indonesia, Giorgio from Italy, Sue from England, David from Lebanon, and Pam from British Guyana. I am struck by the fact that nobody is from France.

It wasn't for lack of trying. Jim had invited numerous French acquaintances, but they had all declined. This was hardly surprising—the French don't celebrate Thanksgiving, but they are also very conservative when it comes to inviting others into their homes for dinner, or to being invited. Ramon explains that French people take a long time to become acquainted on such intimate terms, but I have another theory, and it doesn't apply just to the French. Most people make their friends in childhood. By the time they become adults, there is simply no desire, or need, to search out new ones—they already have all the pals they need, thank you. For people who travel the world, however, taking your friends along is not an option—you must either cultivate new ones or dine alone. We raise a glass, give thanks for our blessings, and toast our new acquaintances.

If Parisians give newcomers short shrift, at least they pay attention to their own past. Hardly a street in the city is without an historical street plaque. Not the subdued kind, like the discrete blue circles in London reminding you that some poet choked to death on a blood sausage at this address in 1896, but shiny marble slabs with gold embossed lettering, affixed to the building with big brass bolts. These, *mon ami*, are plaques as they truly should be.

I first notice this penchant for municipal embellishment while walking through the public marketplace at place Baudoyer, the square in front of the 4th arrondissement *mairie*. There, amid the fresh peppers and the roasting Provençal pork ribs, is a garland of flowers affixed to the front of the local police headquarters. Beside the flowers is a sign commemorating the policemen who died on this spot during the Second World War.

Once I had spotted the first plaque, I began to see hundreds of similar tablets throughout the city. Many are dedicated to the resistance fighters who fell during that momentous week in August 1944, when Paris arose against the German occupying forces. The site of the Gestapo headquarters, on a quiet residential street just off the Champs-Elysées, is marked by a particularly chilling plaque: "In Homage to the Resisters tortured in this house during the Occupation, 1940–44."

In fact, the more plaques I discover, the more I become convinced there is something in the soul of Parisians that demands a grisly theme. The Marais has a series of freestanding, oar-shaped signs embedded in the sidewalks throughout the neighbourhood. In addition to being a good reason to watch where you're going, they educate visitors to the colourful local history. Just around the corner from rue Barbette is a cobbled alleyway, the impasse des Arbalétriers, which winds its way through the bowels of the block. Along the way, it passes a lens-grinding shop and the Swiss Cultural Centre. At the end of the alley is a sign announcing a heinous crime that took place six centuries ago: "On November 23, 1407, Jean-sans-Peur, duke of Burgundy, had his cousin, Louis, the Duke of Orleans, assassinated while the latter was visiting Queen Isabeau at the Hôtel Barbette. This marked the beginning of civil war."

The problem with Paris, of course, is that there is hardly a square metre in the city that hasn't had something nasty happen on it over the last thousand years. One gets the impression that some of the local citizenry, while proud of their heritage, might not mind fewer grisly reminders. My favourite plaque is situated on the tiny rue Sidi Brahim, just west of the bois de Vincennes. Bolted above the doorway on a nondescript building, the slab boldly announces: "Here, on the 17th of April, 1967, Nothing Happened."

The clouds that have wrapped the city in a cold grey ceiling for the last week finally depart on the weekend. It is a beautiful, crisp day, and Linda and I decide to go and see the fall colours at the Musée de la Sculpture en Plein Air. The museum, which is located on the Left Bank of the Seine, just east of Ile Saint-Louis, is a wonderful spot to stroll and admire the mountain ash, weeping willow, and chestnut trees as they trade their summer green for a rich assortment of russet and gold.

A group of dog lovers have set up a dog obedience course on the promenade. It consists of a twelve-point maze, complete with large cartoons showing their expected tricks, presumably for German shepherds who can't understand French. One of the images shows a poodle heeling, while another displays a Labrador faithfully coming to a stop on command. My favourite is the image of a Bouvier obediently lying under a restaurant table while his master eats.

Parisians love their dogs. In fact, they take better care of them than of their own children. I have seen tiny Yorkshire terriers riding along the sidewalk in the baby carriage while a toddler wanders in adjacent traffic. And I have definitely seen many more dogs in restaurants than children.

The Relais de l'Entrecôte is located in the 6th arrondissement, just around the corner from Saint-Germain des Prés church. It is decorated in traditional brasserie trappings, with a bright red awning, gilt-framed mirrors, and nineteenth-century furniture. The waitresses all wear black dresses, white aprons, and bright red lipstick.

The best part of the Relais is that they only serve one dish on the menu, and that is *steak et frites*. The waitress, unfailingly polite, doesn't ask what you want, but how you want it done. Rare is the operative condition, medium is frowned upon, and well done is just, well, "not done here, Monsieur."

A bottle of house red is placed on the table, and the main meal is served. The entrecôte, carefully trimmed of all extraneous matter, is grilled to perfection and sliced into medallions of succulent meat. The plate is piled high with shoe-string frites, fried to crisp, mouth-watering perfection and dusted with the lightest coating of sea salt.

The *pièce de résistance*, the final detail that raises the Relais above all the others, is the sauce. Legend has it that the restaurant is owned by two sisters with an irreconcilable grudge, each accusing the other of stealing the family's secret recipe. I have no idea if the story is true or not, but if there was ever a recipe worthy of theft, this is it. A concoction of butter, beef broth, mustard, and fresh ground pepper is reduced over a low flame until it has the texture of liquid silk and is then poured over the meat. It is enough to make you lick your plate clean and beg for more. And more is what we get.

As soon as we are done, the waitress brings over a hot tray and piles our plate high with seconds. By the time we are finished, the table has moved several inches closer to my tummy. I am told they have an excellent dessert menu of tiramisu, crème brûlée, and profiteroles, but I simply do not have the Gallic fortitude to last that long.

Most of the clientele are customers of long standing, including one woman who shows up every Saturday for lunch dressed in diamonds, with a small Pomeranian. She places the dog on the floor, where it patiently waits for its dinner. The waitress brings out a plate of raw entrecôte approximately the same size as the pooch, but within seconds, the meat has disappeared. The Pomeranian then rests contentedly in its mother's ample lap for the rest of the meal, swollen to the size of a stuffed Hoover bag. When I die, I want to come back as a poodle in Paris.

I am sitting at a café with Jim near the Picasso Museum. It is not a particularly warm day, but Jim is a conscientious smoker and insists on sitting at a table outdoors. I wrap my hands around my coffee as I read *Le Parisien*. The ministry of health has released its eagerly awaited annual survey on the country's bad habits. The imbibing of wine and extramarital affairs are up, it seems, but the consumption of cigarettes is down. Researchers have no ready explanation for this apparent paradox. Perhaps, they theorize, the margin of error is skewing the results.

And perhaps the respondents are just lying. My personal experience—I am referring to smoking, now—would indicate that cigarettes are more popular than ever. Recent bylaws have forced office-bound puffers out onto the streets, where they congregate in tar-stained huddles to litter the sidewalks with yellow, cylindrical debris. During every recess, a large gaggle of teenage girls at the nearby school scurries to the adjacent parkade to strike up their Marlboros. At night, residents on the floors above toss their Gitanes out the window, the butts showering sparks like a comet as they bounce down the walls to the sidewalks below.

Just as Jim stubs out his smoke, a woman approaches our table. "May I have a cigarette?"

Jim shakes his head. "No."

Not at all miffed by the rebuff, she simply approaches the table beside us, where a young woman with a butterfly tattoo on her neck readily complies.

Jim is normally a very generous person, and I am surprised by his response. "Why didn't you give her one yourself?" I ask.

"Because *everyone* in this town bums cigarettes. I was going through a pack a day. I finally decided to just say no."

I turn to the tattooed woman. "Excuse me, but why do you give out cigarettes?"

She puffs on her smoke and ponders my question. "It is a kindness between strangers, a way of affirming that we are all humans, not robots."

"Bullshit," says Jim.

"No, it is true," she continues. "If they approach me with a demand, I will not do it. But if they ask me with a smile, I am happy to give them one."

A good answer, I thought. Perhaps it also explained the statistics, if not for wine, then at least for extramarital affairs.

As November approaches, I am surprised to see Halloween decorations appearing in the shop windows. Although the French have certainly demonstrated a tradition towards headless corpses and disturbed graves, I had never noticed any effort to promote these activities annually. Still, I am happy to see the French having a go at it. Halloween was my favourite religious holiday when I was a child. Not only does it encourage irreverence for the dead, but it also gives adolescents the opportunity to dress up in disguise and extort candy from adults upon pain of vandalism. You've got to work pretty hard to come up with a better combination than that for a youngster.

Unfortunately, adults must leave most of these diversions behind. The one remaining comfort is the ability to wear orange without suffering recrimination. As I cross rue des Archives on my way to the Italian deli, I spot a woman of perhaps sixty years in a purple Lycra body suit, orange trench coat, and long silk scarf in royal purple.

So far, so good. What is unusual is the fact that this woman is strolling arm-in-arm with her exact copy, identically clad. The twin sisters promenade along, chattering away, happy as children on a Saturday morning merry-go-round. I assume they are on their way to a costume party, but in the Marais, you never know.

NOVEMBRE

There is something about the change of seasons that always brings new revelations to the senses. It is my experience, for instance, that you never notice how mouldy a three-hundred-year-old building is until you close the windows. As the chill, damp winds of November blow down from the North Sea, the cobbled foyer of 23, rue Barbette takes on a damp smell, not unlike that of a wet dog that's been rifling through garbage cans in the back alley. In the morning, when I go down to pick up the newspaper, it creeps up the stairwell, trying to sneak into the apartment.

Not that it would have been easy to spot, had it gotten in. Our bathroom, tiled in white and yellow ceramic, had begun to cultivate ominous blooms of black fungus, despite our strenuous efforts to scrub them into oblivion. The shower curtain, in particular, had become an exotic haven for flora and fauna—one particular splotch had a startling, somewhat sinister resemblance to Michael Flatley of Riverdance fame. Linda finally ordered me to replace it.

Reluctantly, I agreed. It isn't that I had any particular attachment to the shower curtain, or to Michael, for that matter. It's just that I had to weigh the odour against Linda's dread of shopping for a new one.

My woeful lack of French had finally caught up to me. It

had been approximately thirty years since I last studied French in high school, and about fifteen years since I had last attempted to brutalize the language orally. I could still handle simple requests, such as, "Where is the toilet?" or, "How much for this ashtray shaped like a beret?" But anything more demanding, such as "I am wiping my foot on your terrier, Madame, because the material on the bottom of my shoe belongs to it," was well beyond my linguistic skill. Suddenly, I realized, I was here for a long time, not just a good time. Would I ever learn French?

Knowing that a beer would not worsen my problem, I head for the Moosehead in search of moral support. When I arrive, I am impressed to see that Mark has managed to find a live broadcast of an NHL game—Toronto Maple Leafs versus Montreal Canadiens—which I think particularly apt for my predicament. Over a cold draft, I ask my host whether he had had a command of the French language before coming over.

"Nope. I failed French in high school. When I got here, I was like a mute."

"How did you get by?"

"I did a lot of smiling and nodding."

"But did folks here react negatively to your lack of French?"

Mark shrugs. "Sometimes they were rude, so I was rude back. That softened them up."

Good advice, at least if you're a hockey player. I order a Maple Dew and ask him how long it took to get comfortable with French.

Mark thinks about it as he mixes the cocktail. "It came to me a lot easier than I expected. The day I knew I was bilingual was when I got into an argument and I didn't think about it, it just came out."

I am heartened by Mark's reassurances, but an incident the next day plants more than a smidgeon of doubt deep into my psyche. I had gone to a bookstore to search for a copy of the *Guide rouge*, Michelin's extensive listing of hotels and restaurants in every city and village in the country. Using my laborious French, I painstakingly ask the clerk if they have any copies in English. "Oh no," he replies in English. "They only publish in French."

I am suddenly filled with dread. Does everyone in Paris really understand English but isn't speaking it to me because it's more fun to watch me sweat blood? Normally I'm very good about things like hallucinations and paranoia. Perhaps, I rationalize, the average Parisian holds his own language in such high regard that he assumes I would be insulted if he spoke anything less than perfect English to me.

Not even I believe that, so I decide to ask a Frenchman. Bernard is a thirty-nine-year-old native of La Rochelle, an ancient port on the Atlantic coast of France. A small, muscular man with short-cropped hair, he spent several years travelling throughout the United States before taking a job at a wine outlet on rue Rambuteau in the Marais.

"No, it's just laziness," he explains when I advance my theory. "Most people in Paris simply don't make the effort to speak English."

Is it still paranoia, I wonder, when they really *do* despise you?

In the meantime, the state of the shower curtain is such that it will bite us if we get too close. Linda orders me off to buy not only the shower curtain, but also a new set of hanging rings. With a heavy sigh, I pull on my coat and venture forth for oral abuse. Taking my trusty little French/English dictionary along, I walk down to BHV, a large department store across from the Hôtel de Ville.

BHV is organized into five floors, with hardware located in the basement and bathroom accessories on the third floor. I decide to start at the bottom. The hardware section is jammed to the brim with all the things a Frenchman might need: slug catchers, wine corkers, industrial garlic presses, and an artificial frog pond. I know this, because I patiently search each aisle in the vain hope that I might stumble upon the motherlode of shower curtain rings and, thus, save myself from ridicule. Alas, the closest things I come up with are the adjustable clamps that fit around car radiator hoses. I briefly toy with the idea of purchasing twelve, but I can't delude myself into thinking that Linda wouldn't notice. Resigned to my fate, I pull out my dictionary with the same enthusiasm Robespierre must have felt as he removed his necktie.

There is no translation for shower curtain rings in my little dictionary; the closest thing I can find is *ronde*, which means circle. Unfortunately, it also means inebriated. I approach a balding man dressed in a green clerk's vest and, in my best patchwork French, announce that I want to get pissed in the bathroom. He gives me a look that suggests some pathetic *anglais* tells him this at least three times a day. "Try the third floor, sir."

I go up to bathroom accessories, again consulting my treacherous dictionary on the way. This time, I will try a different tack, explaining that I want the little rings through which you stick a shower curtain rod. I patch together a sentence using baguette for rod, and *anneau* for ring. I learn later that, with unerring accuracy, I have picked the street slang for dick and asshole, so when I waylay a young, pretty clerk and announce in a loud voice, accompanied by helpful hand signals, that I want to know in which aisle I can sodomize her at a reasonable price, she blushes and runs off.

I eventually manage to find the shower curtain and rod rings before security has the opportunity to march me off to pervert prison. Returning home, I happily show my purchases to Linda. She glances at them once, then sighs the way all women do when they send their husbands off to perform the simplest household chores. "They're the wrong size, dear. You're going to have to take them back."

Fortunately, our experience with making a house into a home is far less onerous than Jim's. When he arrived in Paris, his apartment had no cupboards, fridge, or stove—the previous owners had even taken the kitchen sink. "Oh, that's quite normal in Paris," his agent explained. It took him 100,000 francs and three months before he could fry an egg.

Most of our kitchen was left in place, which is a mixed blessing. Our cooker is a hybrid model, with a gas stove top and an electric oven. In many ways, it resembles the French system of state, which combines all the efficiency of a federal bureaucracy with the flexibility of a unionized workforce. In this case, the gas stove is too hot to prepare anything but molten lead, and the oven can't warm ice cream to a puddle in under three hours. The reason the oven doesn't work is because it has a convection fan that blows all the heat into the kitchen. When I first turned the machine on, a blast of hot air almost peeled the skin off my knees. While it's nice for heating the house up, I can roast a potato on the top shelf for two hours and it's still as hard as a billiard ball.

I would gladly have traded the cooker in for a barbecue. For the last several years, I have been diligently refining my skills on a Weber gas appliance, using it to cook everything from rosemary lamb to eggplant in balsamic vinegar. Not only have I come to love the taste of roasted food, but I also take great delight in tormenting the neighbours with the succulent smells.

Unfortunately, barbecues in Paris are about as common as honest cab drivers. The reasons are two-fold. First, there are no outdoor balconies where such a device can perch. Second, and most important, the average Parisian would just as soon ask a waiter for ketchup as put such a blatantly American affectation on display.

The Maestro's main concession to North American tastes was to supply a brand new clothes washer. It is a German design, and the device does not even remotely resemble a normal washing machine, in form or function. For one thing, when you open the top, the drum inside is designed to tumble *sideways*, like a Ferris wheel for midgets. Inside this drum is enough space to fit three hankies and two pairs of underwear, but only if they are the thong variety.

Our washer has one other peculiarity—once you start it, there is no way to stop it until it's good and ready. I discovered this one day after realizing I had inadvertently left my wallet in a pair of pants. In spite of my best efforts to pry the lid open, it churned merrily along for the next hour, subjecting my credit cards and francs to a Teutonic version of cleanliness.

At least it isn't a combined washer/dryer, which has a further three hundred cycles dedicated to spinning clothes to within an inch of disintegration. Ideally, you load the washer and forget about it, which you will do anyway, as the normal wash/dry cycle is about thirteen hours. It is so slow that, unless you are a life member at a nudist colony, you will never have enough clean clothes.

Why, I wonder, would anyone invent such a cruel and

unusual device? I picture the Krupp family standing in the ruins of their Ruhr appliance factory, shaking their fists at the departing Allied bombers, vowing revenge in the most heinous fashion. Over the following decades, legions of their mechanical offspring march forth to occupy a corner in every laundry room from Red Square to the Arc de Triomphe. Some day the Germans will re-conquer Europe, simply because their foes won't be able to find enough clean clothes to go out the door.

In the meantime, the French have a far more worrisome invasion pending—the Euro. After 1,500 years, the franc is about to succumb to a currency that sounds like a bladder disease. For the last two years, governments all over Europe have been printing and striking some 300 billion coins and notes, and transporting them to banks by armoured car, re-sizing cash tills, training police to spot forgeries, and generally making life miserable for anyone with even a passing association with cash.

The French, of course, don't give a rat's *crotte* for any of it. They couldn't care less if the currency printers went on strike or the banks refused to hand bills out on New Year's Day. No, the average citizen is far more concerned about the contents of his mattress and what to do with them. One of the most cherished secrets of the average Parisian is the amount of cash kept *sous la laine*. The Bank of France estimates that up to 200 billion francs have been squirrelled away in dark little corners, far out of sight of official prying eyes. The problem is that, within a few months, the old currency will no longer be convertible. Every Frenchman must somehow transubstantiate his stash of cash without arousing undue suspicion.

The standard Gallic solution, of course, is to drink it. I am standing in Bernard's wine store when a Range Rover pulls up to the loading zone out front. A middle-aged man with a broken nose and several large gold rings on his fingers enters the store. "You got any champagne?"

"Yes, sir. What kind would you like?"

"The most expensive."

Bernard carries several cases of Veuve Clicquot out to the back of the 4 x 4, and the man produces a thick wad of 500-franc bills. Removing the rubber band holding it together, he peels off a stack of bright green notes and pays for his purchase in cash.

"Who was that?" I ask.

"He runs a whorehouse over in Les Halles."

"Thirsty clients?"

"No, snoopy tax collectors."

I rub my left thumb against my index finger, the universal sign for financial chicanery. "So, he's doing the laundry."

"Maybe." Bernard holds up one of the 500-franc bills, which features a portrait of Madame Curie. "But I like his washerwoman."

Around the middle of November, as I am ascending the steps of the Saint-Paul Metro station, I am greeted by the smell of roasting chestnuts. A young Algerian man in a grey polyester jacket is stationed at the top of the steps. His portable barbecue consists of a five-gallon metal pail filled with charcoal. The bottom of a steel barrel, carefully punctured with holes, has been fitted to the top of the pail. The entire contraption is mounted in a shopping cart, charitably supplied by the local *supermarché*. Judging from the delightful aroma, the chestnuts have been cooking for at least an hour. I purchase a bag and munch on them as I head home. The tough outer skins have split, and the interiors are soft, sweet, and chewy.

Street selling in Paris is a time-honoured tradition. Along the busy rue de Rivoli, salesmen in plywood booths hawk everything from carrot slicers to nylon socks. At the corner adjacent to the BHV, a man with a gas-fired griddle will even whip up a chocolate and strawberry crepe for you while you wait.

There are, of course, street sellers of the more larcenous sort. As I head down to the wine shop later that afternoon, Jean-Pierre, his green baseball cap askew, stops me on the street. "Hey, Canada! I got something for you!" He opens up a very large plastic shopping bag to reveal at least a hundred DVDs and videos, all slightly the worse for wear and tear.

I stare in wonderment. "Where did you get these?"

At that moment, an elderly white-haired woman on the arm of a substantial Haitian matron passes us on their morning constitutional. "He pinched them from the flea market," she answers. "He's been doing it for years."

"Shh!" Jean-Pierre smiles, embarrassed, and holds his finger to his lips. He turns to me. "Look, they are in English. I have the entire video collection of Black Adder—would you like to buy it? I'll give you a special price."

How appropriate: one old scoundrel promoting another. I decline, not wishing to inadvertently join one of the city's oldest professions, fencing stolen goods.

The old woman has no such compunctions. "Got anything with Richard Gere? He's hot." I leave the two of them rummaging through the bag, deep in pursuit of a deal.

When I arrive at the wine shop, I am greeted by a sign announcing the imminent arrival of Beaujolais Nouveau Day. In the United Kingdom, they honour Guy Fawkes, a spy who tried to blow up Parliament with kegs of gunpowder. In Mexico, they march to the graveyards and tidy up the dead on All Saints Day. In France, for the last fifty years, they have been celebrating the first taste of Beaujolais on the third Thursday in November. Of the three, I go for Beaujolais Nouveau Day. Not only is it more relevant than these other celebrations, but it also tastes better.

Preparations for BN Day actually begin in September, when workers handpick Gamay grapes from the vine. The grapes are crushed and mixed with a yeast that ferments quickly. After one month of settling in the barrel, the wine is bottled and shipped worldwide for its date with the world's palates.

When I inform Linda and Jim that BN Day is nigh, I am given marching orders to pick a selection for tasting on the designated day. This involves going from wine store to wine store, where the owners have set up *dégustations*. My first stop is Bernard's wine cellar, where he has cheerfully uncorked half a dozen selections and set them atop a barrel outside his door. "They are a little too cool for tasting, but I think you will enjoy them," he explains as he pours the first sample.

The proper way to taste is to take a sip, swill it around in your mouth, and then spit it into a bucket supplied for that purpose. I obligingly swish a Beaujolais Villages Nouveau and am greeted by the distinct flavour of bananas. "That's the special yeast," explains Bernard. I try a few more wines and their taste ranges from mild and thin to powerful and full bodied. As with all Nouveau, the price runs from 25 to 40 francs per bottle. I select four.

My next stop is Nicolas, an ubiquitous chain store. The outlet in our neighbourhood is run by the French equivalent of Lucille Ball, and I am always hesitant about subjecting myself to the logic of a French redhead, but this time Natalie is orbiting relatively close to Earth, and I have no problem picking out two delightful bottles from her selection.

As I head home, I pass a store which specializes in wines from the Côtes du Rhône. I have never been in there, but the interior of the shop is filled with happy, red-faced people, which I take to be a good sign in a wine shop. A table of cheese, bread, and pâtés has been set out, and the *caviste* is holding court around a dozen bottles of wine. "You must try this!" is his favourite expression.

Over the course of the day, I have tried my best to stick to the accepted method of "sip and spit," but this particular establishment has opened several bottles of vintage Côtes du Rhône in the 250 francs range, which buys you a nice gargle in France, and I am loath to spit it out. I quickly begin to understand why everyone is so cheerful. In addition to the Nouveau and the upscale tipple, the *caviste* has set up a wine barrel with a tap so that everyone can simply help themselves when their glasses get too low. Although I don't quite remember the details, I end up buying several more bottles of wine.

That evening, Linda and Jim are quite impressed with the selection, and we choose four to taste. After our *dégustation*, we retire to Camille's, a nearby brasserie, where the patrons are lined up out the door, eager to taste the restaurant manager's personal selection of Nouveau. We have a wonderful, château-bottled Gamay with our meal of *foie gras*, *rumsteak* and *frites*, and—it is rather hazy by this time—crème brûlée for dessert.

Before coming to France, I had been under the impression that Beaujolais Nouveau Day was a cynical marketing ploy to get people to drink under-aged, over-priced wine. The truth is, the French don't need much of an excuse to knock back wine. Regardless of the quality, BN Day is a big fete that

Parisians embrace with a passion and look forward to celebrating every year. They can count me in.

Mark, a friend of ours from Calgary, is taking a late fall break to visit France. Since he has already been to Paris and has seen all the major tourist sites, I try to think of something different to show him.

November, of course, is a fine month for visiting cemeteries. The weather is too inclement for the crowds, but not too cold to deter lingering. In addition to the Catacombs, with its thousands of stacked skeletons, and Montparnasse (current address of Jean-Paul Sartre and Simone de Beauvoir), there is Père Lachaise. Oscar Wilde, just before he passed away in a Paris hotel in 1900, is said to have looked up from his deathbed at the ghastly wallpaper decorating his room. "One of us has to go," he announced. The wallpaper remained and the dramatist promptly decamped to Père Lachaise.

During the cold months, the narrow lanes that meander through the resting places of Père Lachaise are lightly populated with a sprinkling of mourners and voyeurs. The sun slants through the bare limbs of tall chestnut trees and a not-unpleasant smell of soil and decaying floral wreaths hangs in the still air, striking just the right olfactory note for a necropolis. Wilde is tucked up in the north end, beneath a rather futuristic monument designed by Jacob Epstein. The stone carving features a naked, vaguely Egyptian figurine wearing a space helmet and a flying backpack, the significance of which eludes me, but no doubt would have evinced pride in Wilde's iconoclastic breast.

In addition to Edith Piaf and Yves Montand, Père Lachaise boasts another famous singer. Jim Morrison died in a Paris hotel bathtub in 1971 during his exile from America over an incident involving on-stage exposure. I think that Wilde would have approved the gesture.

Mark decides that he would much rather see the Musée d'Orsay, not that I mind in the least. It has one of the finest collections of art in the world, including works by Renoir, Cézanne, and Van Gogh. Mark's favourite display is the art nouveau furniture on the middle floor. For several decades before the First World War, designers and architects created a movement that embodied the fluid expressions of nature into furniture, jewellery, and glassware. Some of the finest examples, including a wooden bed frame that flows across the floor and up the wall to a height of 4.5 metres, capture the spirit and vitality of the artistic movement.

My favourite is the quartet of paintings that Monet did of Rouen Cathedral. The works depict the same view in varying conditions of light and shadow. They are mere shadows—impressions—of the high-Gothic façade, but they showcase the artist's brilliant command of his medium more than any other works.

On the way home from the musée, we bump into another well-known Paris artist—the pickpocket. We are standing in a Metro train as it rattles along eighteen metres below the rue de Rivoli. Just as we reach the Châtelet station, I feel a hand in my pocket. Since both of my own are currently occupied holding onto a handrail, I am immediately suspicious. I turn and confront a well-dressed man in his late twenties who is studiously staring off into the distance, seemingly unaware that his hand is inside someone else's pants.

"Pickpocket!" I shout, inadvertently stumbling upon the

French nomenclature. The man's eyes go wide, and he and a second man bolt through the open doors and disappear among the crowds on the platform.

I learn later that most professional thieves work the subway system in pairs. They prefer the #1 Metro line, which has a plethora of tourists, presumably carrying lots of cash and ignorant of the dangers. The pickpockets normally target a victim near the doors. That's where it's most crowded, and people's hands are occupied holding onto the railing. While the accomplice shields the action with a bag or coat, the pickpocket unzips a purse or lifts the victim's coattails in preparation for the theft. As the train pulls into the station, the pickpocket makes his dip, quickly handing the wallet to his accomplice in case of detection. As the doors open, they dodge off the train and blend into the crowds. Once they reach ground level, they pull out any cash and throw the wallet (and credit cards) into the trash.

Fortunately, I had placed my wallet in a front pocket. Just as the train was pulling up to the station, I had shifted my weight forward, inadvertently trapping the thief's thumb between my wallet and thigh. Realizing his blunder, he had let go of the wallet and run.

As soon as I assure myself that my money is safe, I look around for some help. Two women police officers are standing not 4.5 metres farther down in the car. "A man just tried to steal my wallet! He got off at the Châtelet."

The two look at me, bored. "You will have to get a form from the commissioner."

I want to ask them to lend me a pair of handcuffs so that I can just catch him for them, but I decide I'd already had my lucky break for the day and not to go fishing for another.

I am quickly learning that Paris is unlike any other place on Earth, for a very simple reason. In North America, the day is spliced into predictable, pre-packaged doses, with everyone isolated in their car, their mall, or their suburban box. In Paris, when you walk out the door, you don't know what you're going to encounter—cherry blossoms, riot patrols, or Chinese lanterns hanging on the lampposts. The day springs to life as a full-blown performance, and if you are not part of the audience, you are part of the cast.

As I am sitting in my living room writing this down, the apartment reverberates with strange music emanating from the street below. Going to the window, I spy an organ grinder coming up the street. As he passes the school, the kids standing out front pull the Walkman plugs from their ears and begin to dance along the sidewalk, like monkeys in Nikes. I recognize the tune as "God Rest Ye Merry Gentlemen" and realize, with a start, that Christmas is only a few weeks away. I head down to street level to investigate further

The organ grinder, named Michel, is accompanied by a man in a torn leather jacket with a nose that has been flattened by a blunt instrument—a tire iron, I suspect. He is mute, but then, I don't think he is there for conversation. Some organ grinders still employ a monkey to scramble up the drainpipes on the front of apartments to collect coins. However, there had been reports in the news that teenagers were robbing buskers, so perhaps Michel had traded in his monkey for a gorilla. I get the impression that Michel doesn't get robbed much with this man in tow.

Michel himself is in his forties and sports a grey fedora and a perpetual cigarette between his lips. Between puffs, he explains he has lived in Paris all his life and has been playing the *orgue* on street corners for over twenty years, since he inherited the instrument from his father.

The *orgue* is a wooden box mounted on tiny rubber wheels with a hand crank on the left side. Michel is reluctant to explain the machinations too carefully, but, at my urging, and for a 10-franc coin, he opens up the hinged cover on top to reveal a slot about the size of an old eight-track tape. Taking one of a half-dozen cassettes from a rack in the box, he swaps the old song for a new one. He bids adieu, his hand stiff and strong from years of cranking, and they continue on their way, seeking out a new audience and a few francs around the next corner.

DÉCEMBRE

Have you ever noticed how a raw oyster in your mouth feels just like French-kissing a six-month-old calf?

Right up until this moment in my life, I have successfully avoided ingesting oysters, having always viewed them as a form of sea-going slug, but since I've been eating the land-bound version in garlic butter for the last several months, I can no longer hide behind that particular culinary bias. As a consequence, I have been summarily dispatched by my better half to fetch home a dozen *huîtres*.

Overnight, makeshift tables covered with crates of crab and platters of prawns have sprung up on the sidewalks around the Marais, filling the damp December air with the scent of the sea. I am standing at the roadside emporium of a Breton fishmonger on rue Rambuteau. He has a low, sloping forehead and the general demeanor of a man who would much rather be off somewhere committing acts of piracy. Having dutifully found the offered sample sufficiently oleaginous for human consumption, I hand him a large, shallow bowl. He fills the bottom with ice and a layer of kelp, and then begins to shuck the hapless mollusks with a sinister knife that has appeared from his sleeve. Placing the tip of the short blade directly behind the oyster's hinge, he pries it back and forth for a moment until the shapeless form inside gives up its grip. He then slides the blade in farther and pries the top shell off completely, revealing a naked, gelatinous creature resting in a pearly bed. Within a minute or so, he shucks the entire lot, adds a complementary lemon, and *bon appétit*. I head back home, wishing I had one tenth his facility with a shiv and thinking what a fine word oleaginous is.

By the time I arrive home, Linda has set out the official bivalve cutlery. Using a tiny, two-pronged fork, I pry the foot of the oyster off the bottom of the shell and spoon a dollop of red wine vinegar and shallot dressing on top. Then, lifting the shell to my lips, I slurp the whole oyster into my mouth.

For me to say that the experience is like kissing a young cow is not entirely fair. I have come to this conclusion dishonestly because I have, in fact, never been that intimate with the bovine species. But if I had, then I bet it would definitely be right up there in the same league with the #3 Normandy currently negotiating my esophagus.

The taste, however, is something else entirely. The natural brine within the oyster shell mixes with the red wine vinegar and shallots to create a cocktail that bathes the oyster in a velvety glow. It is a maritime symphony, a sublime, crustacean caress of the tongue. We raise our glasses of Crémant and make a toast: "Here's to the bravest man in the world, the first one to eat a raw oyster."

As the month advances, the big department stores begin to fill their windows with festive displays. On a blustery Saturday, we take the Metro to La Samaritaine, which has decorated its large street-side windows with dozens of automata. Pretty female dolls clad in green conical hats and bright red cloaks fly on broomsticks over tiny Bethlehem villages as the surprised—

and no doubt confused—inhabitants gaze skyward. Try as hard as I might, I don't recall any particular Christmas tradition that features Sabrina, the Teenage Witch, but it's the thought that counts. I can't help but imagine that any unauthorized flights over Bethlehem these days would be met with anti-aircraft fire.

We continue on to Printemps, another of Paris's main cathedrals to commercialism, which has eschewed the puppets and concentrated instead on separating shoppers from the contents of their wallets with a stunning visual display. The immense plane trees that ring the entire block have been strung with tens of thousands of tiny red lights; their trunks sparkle like lamé dresses of bright, cold rubies. The effect is magnificent, and my only disappointment is that the department store refuses to sell me a chainsaw when I make enquiries in the hardware section. They don't believe me when I tell them it is for my mother.

Suitably chilblained, we return to the Marais and head for our local restaurant, Camille's. Located on the corner of rue des Francs-Bourgeois and rue Elzévir, it is a classic French *brasserie*, a homey, unpretentious restaurant with a menu printed each day on a chalkboard. The house wine is invariably a young Beaujolais, such as a Brouilly or Morgon, personally picked by the manager and decanted from a large barrel in the cellar during the hours before supper.

I am intrigued by the name of the restaurant. Does it pay homage to Camille Claudel, the sculptress who became Auguste Rodin's mistress? Even though she broke up with Rodin and went bonkers after he bronzed her bum in an unflattering manner, the allusion has a rather appetizing flair.

According to Patrick, the manager, however, the restaurant is named after the French revolutionary Camille Desmoulins. A young lawyer with a bad stutter but a rapier pen, his pamphlets stirred up the Paris population to the point of attacking and destroying the Bastille. He became a leading light in the revolution until a trip to the guillotine cut short his legal career, among other things. According to witnesses, his farewell speech was very moving, if a little long.

Wrapping a scarf around my neck to ward off the breeze that blows through a gap in the windows, we take a table near the back of the room, the better to observe our fellow diners. People-watching is a popular spectator sport in France. You quickly become adept at recognizing who is the tourist and who the French local. There is a third category, foreigners living in Paris, but they are not considered very interesting.

I spot a widow of a certain age who comes in every evening for dinner. She is dressed in a long, black wool coat with a collar made of light brown fur. Her hair, which is dyed orange and curled into tight swirls, is arranged around her face as artfully as possible under the circumstances. Her lips are painted bright red, and her eyes are lined with blue eyeshadow. At her feet rests a small Pekinese. The dog looks as though he has suffered a significant loss of personal self-esteem at the hands of a fire hydrant, but he is nonetheless very attentive, partly because he is about to eat dinner and partly, no doubt, because he matches the fur trim on mommy's coat.

Steak tartar is created by mixing ground beef with a raw egg, Worcester sauce, Tabasco, and salt and pepper, then mushing the entire concoction together into a patty. Frankly, I am afraid to eat it, but evidently this is not the way the little old doll and her dog feel. The waiter arrives and, with a great flourish, places a large plate of tartar in front of the dowager and a small bowl on the floor for her pet. Within seconds, their plates are clean.

Our waiter approaches to take our order. Dressed in the traditional black vest and white apron and sporting a fine selection of facial scars, he goes by the nickname of Miam-Miam, which roughly translates as "yum-yum." He is always very attentive, teasing us about our pronunciation and congratulating us when we make a good choice, which is difficult not to do because practically everything on the menu is delicious.

He holds up the menu slate. For starters, we order the *haricots* salad. At Camille's, the chef prepares a mix of fresh green beans braised in garlic and olive oil and then mixes in tiny cubes of *foie gras*. The combination is sublime and makes a meal in itself, but for the true Parisian, it is only the beginning.

The main courses always include a selection of grilled sausage, lamb, fish, and beef. The sausage is invariably andouillette, a Lyonnaise concoction of pig guts fried with onions, which tastes exactly as it sounds. Beef, usually sirloin but occasionally tenderloin, is always cooked rare or medium rare—never well done. I have seen Miam-Miam bend over and examine the feet of customers who order their beef in such fashion, solicitously inquiring if they have a hole in the bottom of their shoe that needs repairing. We order the lamb chops, which are grilled in rosemary, pepper, and thyme, and served with roasted potatoes.

Both the starters and the main course are very filling, and when Miam-Miam comes to inquire about dessert, we are sorely tempted. The dessert menu features two standards: crème brûlée and chocolate mousse. The crème brûlée is custard that has had its surface braised with a blowtorch to achieve a brown translucent glaze of sugar, which I think is an excellent application of compressed gas. The mousse, made from buttery cocoa and thick cream, dances across the tongue like a chocolate fairy. Fortunately, desserts don't have any calories at Christmas, so we have one of each.

After the meal, Patrick brings our coats and escorts us to the door, wishing us a happy holiday. We scurry down rue Elzévir toward home. As we turn the corner onto rue Barbette, the wind dies, and a cloud of white flecks dances around the wrought-iron street lamp hanging above. It has started to snow.

By morning, the snow has departed, except for a few specks that cower like fugitives beneath the vacant benches in the Carnavalet museum garden. As the days progress, the people of the Marais gradually pull a similar disappearing act, until the streets take on the appearance of Chernobyl. Not that we suspect a similar cause. The French simply view Christmas as a time to be with family. Plans are made to return to the ancestral farm or the village estate as soon as the school year ends and holidays begin. Ramon is off to Beaune, and Bernard is returning to La Rochelle.

Our friends, as well, begin to plot similar diasporas. David and Pam are going to British Guyana to visit her family. Jim announces that, after a brief business detour to Houston, he is going to stay with his brother in Winnipeg. It looks like we are going to spend Christmas in Paris alone. This means it is time to give our home a little holiday spirit.

Christmas trees are as popular in France as they are in North America, only smaller, and most flower shops around the Marais carry a stock. They are grown near Santa's village in Finland, then cut, wrapped in a plastic-mesh condom, and shipped by the truckload to the wholesale flower markets on the outskirts of Paris. They are mostly fir trees, some with a thick coating of artificial snow that looks about as authentic as a coating of Dream Whip.

I go to see Assam, our florist on rue Rambuteau. Assam's habitual winter gear consists of a thick blue wool coat, a Kanga beret, and a scratchy shadow of beard. Although he is from Morocco, he follows traditional French small-business finances, which is to put all bills of debt in the right pocket and all cash, i.e., nothing the taxman will ever find, in the left.

Assam's family has been in the floral business for three generations, and he invariably has the freshest stock of roses, tulips, and irises in the neighbourhood. His tiny shop is barely one metre wide—it is literally a disused stairwell to the building above—and the interior is crammed with dozens of tin buckets, each one holding thick bouquets of lilies, gerbera, and sunflowers, a riot of colours, smells, and textures. Each day, he carries the buckets out to the sidewalk, carefully arranging them in the tiny public space appropriated for his commerce.

His selection of trees, looking like furry green lollipops, is stacked in a pile outside on the sidewalk. I wonder what a North African Muslim must think of this ritual fetish for tiny evergreens, but set the theological implications aside as we rummage through the pile. I choose a particularly fresh-smelling specimen about one metre high, and Assam brings out a large hammer and affixes a wooden cross to the bottom of the trunk, which will serve as a base for the duration of the holidays.

Decorating the tree is a problem. All of our lights and ornaments are back in Calgary, packed in storage. I first try to enliven the tree with thin strands of gold tinsel, but it ends up looking like Cousin It in *The Addams Family*. I next apply some red, white, and blue foil garlands, but now the tree resembles a reject from Bastille Day. Finally, I break down and go to BHV to buy a string of multi-coloured lights. The clerk, a cheery woman with bright rosy cheeks, recommends a string of gold, blue, and red, with an electronic control with eight flash settings. It is, I note, manufactured in that bastion of Christianity, China.

I take my purchase home and string it around the tree. After studying the control, which offers such delights as twinkly/flashflash and steadyon, I choose the setting least likely to induce epileptic convulsions. After several eggnogs, my feeling of nausea begins to dissipate, and the lights actually begin to twinkle in time to the Barbra Streisand Christmas CD on our stereo. I don't know if Barbra planned it that way, but the tree looks quite merry keeping a visual beat to "O Tannenbaum."

Why is it that Christmas isn't Christmas without a roast turkey? It's not like the baby Jesus sat up in his crib and petted one in his manger. There's no way the Virgin Mary would have let such a miserable creature within a kilometre of her kid. When Linda was a little girl, a turkey at her grandfather's farm once plucked the buttons from her coat and then started on her eye. When I was visiting my Uncle Louis's turkey farm in Saskatchewan, three hundred turkeys stampeded over my little sister. Now, does that sound like an appropriate meal for a holiday dedicated to peace and understanding? I blame the international cranberry cartel for foisting what is essentially an ornery dodo bird with a wrinkly chin on unsuspecting Yuletide celebrants.

Regardless, we set out on a hunting expedition for all the trimmings. Since our little fridge is entirely incapable of holding champagne and even so much as a turkey egg at the same time, we have to time our purchase for Christmas Eve. Fortunately, we find a butcher shop that is open on the twenty-fourth, and we order a turkey for pickup that afternoon.

Finding squash, the only food that comes with its own cooking instructions built into its name, is an easier task. On the Thursday before Christmas, we walk over to the Bastille, where an open-air market stretches for several blocks along the broad, tree-lined promenade of rue Richard Lenoir.

The Bastille market always has a festive, anarchic air, but at Christmas the liveliness is amplified by an order of magnitude. A busker with a thick black beard and a Meerschaum pipe plays strange Swedish chorales on his accordion. A female clerk behind the counter at a tripe shop dances with a tiny, pink-plush piggy toy. Everywhere you look, bunting and crèches compete for attention with stacks of Mandarin oranges, plucked ducks in tinsel booties, and bread loaves baked in the shape of Saint-Joseph.

Even if we didn't need squash, I would have gone to the market anyway, just for the sheer pleasure of watching Parisians shop. An African greengrocer hollers to all concerned that he has the sweetest watermelons in the entire city. A balding man in an eiderdown puff coat, bulging like a sausage, stops at the counter to inspect the goods. "Hey, what's this?"

"It's a watermelon."

"But the flesh is yellow! What kind of melon is yellow?"

"A yellow watermelon."

"Fah! What is it, genetically modified? It looks like plastic."

"No, just melon."

"Oh, *merde*, give me half."

I patiently wait my turn and am rewarded by a tiny woman, no taller than 1.2 metres, running over my toes with a shopping cart full of cabbage as she pushes her way to the front of the line. I finally catch the greengrocer's attention by lobbing my squash, rugby style, over the scrum.

Finding cranberry sauce is a different matter. You have about as much chance of finding a can of whale blubber in a French grocery store as you do a jar of this red jelly. After working my way down rue de Rivoli in a fruitless search, I stop for a rest in the tiny park adjacent to the Saint-Paul Metro station.

Jean-Pierre is at his traditional spot in front of the station, enthroned upon a large chunk of foam rubber that protects his posterior from the cold cement steps. Someone has given him a red velvet cap to wear. With his unshaven cheeks, bright red nose, and gap-toothed grin, he looks like Santa's no-good brother, Bert. "Hey, Canada! *Joyeux Noël.*"

"Merry Christmas," I reply, rather dispiritedly.

"Why so glum?"

I don't even know the French word for cranberry, so I have to explain my problem in English.

To my surprise, Jean-Pierre immediately recognizes the ingredient. "That is the red sauce for turkey, yes?" A man of many talents, he helpfully points me in the direction of the rue Charles V, where I eventually locate a grocery store called, of all things, Thanksgiving. The proprietor, bless her Yankee heart, has gone to the trouble of ordering in a large supply of cranberry sauce and is more than happy to sell a can to a desperate sauce junkie for the ludicrous sum of 40 francs.

One last necessity remains on our list: liquid refreshments. The traditional Christmas drink in France, of course, is champagne. Invented by monks in the Champagne district in the fourteenth century, it was kept a well-guarded secret for about fifteen minutes. After that, all the other wine-growing regions began bottling it at a furious rate, but they were not allowed to call it champagne, under threat of disembowelment. Thus inspired, they invented a slew of synonyms, including *pétillant* and *crémant*.

Perhaps it's all the pirates, bishops, and bastards in my lineage, but I must confess, I prefer sparkling rosé to champagne. Not the vile stuff that you would get your older cousin to purchase from the liquor store, the one that goes so well with Fritos, but real sparkling rosé from the Loire or Alsace. I can state from personal observation that every corner grocery store in Paris carries at least half a dozen different brands from all corners of France, all priced at one-quarter the cost of champagne, and all just as tasty. My favourite is *Crémant de Loire*, which originates in the region around Chinon, an ancient château near Orleans. We had purchased a case, along with a special device for opening sparkling wines. It is called a "universal tool" and resembles a large pair of pliers. I suppose you could use it for any number of chores, including firmly but gently immobilizing the cranium of a gerbil while brushing its teeth, but it is plainly meant for opening corks. Don't want to risk carpal tunnel syndrome, do we?

There is one invariable rule about the Marais, and that is *nothing ever goes as planned.* The day before Christmas, we arrive at the *boucher* to pick up our turkey. Somewhere along the line, however, the staff has managed to screw up our order for a five-kilogram bird, and all they have left is a fifteen-kilogram monster the size of a ride-em lawnmower. The butcher is very apologetic and offers to sell it to us for the cut-rate price of 350 francs, head still attached. We decline, reluctant to pay so much for a bird that can still look you in the eye as you stuff its behind with breadcrumbs. We scramble down rue de Rivoli, praying that Monoprix still has some stock on hand.

Fortunately, the grocery store has a large selection of poultry. We purchase an admirable turkey, *sans tête*. We cart it home, happy at last to put up our feet, pour a glass of bubbly, and wait for Santa to come down the chimney.

Christmas Day arrives cold, damp, and overcast. It rarely snows in Paris, which is just as well, as the city's drivers would respond by maniacally crashing into one another, but even a tiny dusting would have been nice. I open one of the windows in our living room and stick my head out. It is quiet—too quiet. There is never a moment in the Marais when you cannot hear a horn blaring, a scooter revving, a schoolchild screaming blue murder, or a garbage truck rattling up the lane. It feels like the first morning in the world.

We stick the turkey into the oven and put some carols on the stereo. Madame Greco stops by on her way to mass to wish us a Merry Christmas. We give her our *étrenne*, which is a gift of cash for her services during the year.

Etrenne is a European custom that has been raised to an art form by the French. You are expected to give cash to all of the people who serve you throughout the year, including the mailman and the street sweeper. This is all very illegal, but everyone does it. The garbagemen come around to each door and hand you a saints' calendar, for which you either pay 100 francs or expect some unfortunate spillage in the coming months.

Another custom that is strictly followed is tipping the fireman for non-emergencies. They don't expect anything for putting out a fire—after all, that's their job—but you'd better stump up if they rush across town to pull your cat off the proverbial hot-tin roof.

David and Pam live in Neuilly-sur-Seine, a suburb just

west of Paris. Their apartment is a beautiful, nineteenth-century building, complete with a marble foyer and a circular staircase that winds up to the large, double doors of their entrance. Just before Christmas, Pam was standing on the landing talking with a friend when a gust of wind closed the door behind her. Pam, without a key, was locked out. Normally this wouldn't be a problem—she could simply wait for Dave to return home—but their five-year-old boy was inside by himself. She called the fire department, which rushed over and raised a ladder to the second floor, broke a window, and clambered through, much to the delight of their son. But not to David's delight. Not only did he end up paying over 500 francs to fix the window, the six *pompiers* expected a tip of 50 francs each for their troubles. He wisely paid up, wishing them *bonne fête*.

Dinner that afternoon is delicious—the turkey is brown and juicy, the mashed potatoes are creamy, and the dressing is a delight. We raise our sparkling rosé and toast all our absent friends, wishing them a Merry Christmas.

Jim arrives back in town shortly thereafter. His friend Heri has just returned from Jakarta, and Jim decides to throw a dinner party to celebrate his first New Year's Eve in Paris.

For the French, organizing a dinner party in Paris is akin to marching on Moscow, only with more provisions. Getting into the spirit of things, Jim visits the butcher who, in addition to supplying a huge roast beef, also recommends some spicy chorizo *saucisse*, rabbit terrine, and dainty *foie gras* for appetizers. I am only surprised he doesn't extol kidney ice cream for dessert.

A few minutes before we arrive, Heri manages to plug up

the kitchen sink and is promptly dispatched to find a plunger. We are greeted at the door by the sight of Jim busily working a coat hanger around the drain, perhaps theorizing that whatever is lurking down there might prefer to hang itself back up in the closet.

"Have a look to see if there's a trap," I offer.

We check under the sink and, sure enough, there is an access plug in the line. Unlike North American U-bends, the French version features an appendixlike attachment below the pipe with a screw-on bottom. We place a tiny fruit bowl beneath the trap and then twist off the cap. Like a big gob of toothpaste, a wide, gelatinous plug of grease, hair, and turkey stuffing comes oozing out.

We are about to congratulate each other on our cleverness when three gallons of filthy water come pouring out into the fruit bowl, splashing upwards like a lawn sprinkler. We scramble to stem the tide by jamming a dishrag into the sink, but by the time we finally stop the flow, the kitchen floor is submerged in a flood of greasy water. Fortunately, Heri returns just in time to grab a mop and benefit from our supervision. Except for the fact that our trousers are soaked to the knees, you can hardly tell there has been a problem, and we soon have the meal on the table.

Naturellement, one doesn't celebrate New Year's Eve in France without the proper libations. The local wine store has been more than happy to supply Jim with enough Pouilly Fuissé, Pomerol, and Piper-Heidsieck to float a battleship. Jim, with admirable foresight, simply brings the lot out to the dining room and opens them on the sideboard, supposing that if you sample enough of everything, the food would find its right wine eventually. I am particularly fond of Château Montbazillac, a sweet white wine from the Dordogne, with the *foie gras*.

By the time midnight approaches, we have reached a state of intoxication during which fighting our way downtown on public transportation with a quarter million drunken Frenchmen sounds like a good idea. We merrily don our coats, hats, and gloves and march out the door.

The subway system in Paris is free during New Year's Eve, an innovation that was instituted a decade ago in an effort to reduce the incidence of cars wrapping themselves around roadside trees. The all-night Metro also supplies free accommodation to the street people who populate the city. When we descend to the #9 line, a fat hobo sporting a tartan dress and corn curls is relaxing on a steel bench with a can of Bud, reading the evening paper. We wish him a *bonne fête*.

In addition to being a perpetual parade ground for Russian mafiosi, the Champs-Elysées is also the social heart of the country. On Bastille Day, thousands of spectators come down to witness the military parade and view their elected representatives before they go to jail. The Tour de France, a twenty-one-day bike race that consumes every paved kilometre and performance-enhancing drug in the country, ends here. And on New Year's Eve, when the rest of the country are snug in their living rooms watching TV, 250,000 revellers are guzzling champagne, firing off Roman candles, and kissing everyone in sight. Twice.

When we emerge onto the Champs-Elysées, night has turned into day. The trees that line the boulevard for two kilometres are ablaze with white lights, and the immense Ferris wheel at Concorde is frenetically flashing its neon cladding. Curiously, there are no rock bands playing on stage, there is no recorded music blaring out of immense speakers—there isn't even an itinerant accordionist belting out a waltz. At the Hôtel de Ville, the city has set up a huge sound system to entertain the crowds as they circle the skating rink (nice touch that, mixing a slippery surface, razor sharp shoes, ABBA, and alcoholic beverages). But the Champs is quiet. I later learn that, at the very same moment that we are gathering in the Champs, rioters in the Paris suburbs, no doubt inflamed by Dick Clark, are setting fire to cars. Presumably, the authorities don't want Louis Vuitton to become an impromptu Roman candle as well.

It is still a few minutes before midnight and I take the opportunity to check out the revellers. Most are young, inebriated, and very happy. From their accents, they seem to be from Australia, Germany, Spain, and North America. For a moment, I wonder if no self-respecting Parisian would ever be seen dead on the Champs on New Year's Eve when a long conga line of people singing French songs comes snaking by. Just shy, I guess.

Precisely at the stroke of midnight, thousands of champagne corks pop in unison as Parisians toast one another. The police, several hundred of whom are on hand in riot gear, completely ignore the liquor infractions, content to smile and sing along, happy to see that the crowd is in a joyous mood. Gradually, the throng disperses toward place de la Concorde, where kids hop into the fountain that marks the spot where Louis XVI was executed. You would never accuse Parisians of being overly tidy, but in a curious display of civic duty, most revellers deposit their bubbly bottles in piles around lampposts—several piles reach a height of two metres—rather than flinging them through the plate-glass windows of Charles Jourdan. Civilized, these French.

JANVIER

My New Year's resolution is to get my testicles to re-descend. This is not a traditional declaration of mine, like giving up purple alcoholic drinks with parasols. Instead, it is a new one, instigated by events that began at 3 AM on New Year's Day.

I had woken up in the middle of the night to discover that the power in our apartment had gone out. Struggling with a flashlight, I finally located the electric box—the master fuse switch had disconnected. Pushing it back into place, I was rewarded with a brief flicker from the hall light before the apartment once again plunged into darkness. After several futile attempts to re-set the switch, I finally went back to bed, muttering about dubious French wiring.

The next morning, at 7 AM, I once again try the switch. This time, it resets without any problem, and the power comes back on in our apartment. I feel very relieved until I step into the shower stall and treat myself to a glacial downpour.

Fortunately, Ramon is staying in the Maestro's apartment next door. Through my chattering teeth and high-pitched voice, he finally figures out that there is no hot water in our apartment. I also explain the mysterious power failure of the night before, wondering if the two might be related.

Ramon swings into action. Calling the electrician on his cellphone, he positions himself in front of the fuse box.

Together, they walk through a lengthy process of flicking switches and muttering, until a diagnosis is finally reached. "The hot water heater is *en panne*," he announces.

"*En panne?*"

"Yes, how you say?" Ramon purses his lips. "*Phute*."

I should have guessed. In Canada, water heaters only go *phute* on the coldest day of the year. Why should it be any different in France? Ramon makes several more phone calls, finally rounding up a plumber willing to do the repair. "You are in luck. We can have it replaced by Saturday." Since it is only Monday, I have to wonder what "unlucky" would have been.

The first month of the year is not the most attractive time in Paris, weather-wise. No troubadour has ever written a ballad about standing on the banks of the Seine and kissing his lover's runny nose. Paris in January is to be endured as much as possible. Take away hot water and you end up with a very unhappy Parisian.

For the next three days, we take our baths in the kitchen, warming up a pot of water on the gas stove and then pouring it into the sink. The only consolation is the warm blast of hot air from the oven as it warms up my derrière.

I certainly don't get much comfort from David. "When did they say the plumber is coming?"

"Saturday."

"Hah. Good luck. I've been waiting three months for them to show up and fix my leaky toilet."

Thank God we have the Euro to provide a distraction. As promised by Brussels and as delivered, to everyone's amazement, the European Union has rolled out its new currency.

Overnight, billions of Deutsch marks, francs, lira, and escudos have been replaced by a single set of shiny new coins.

And nobody has a clue what they're worth. For the last twelve months, stores have had to post dual prices, and every citizen of France has been buying his carrots at either 25 francs per kilogram, or 3.7936267 Euros, after rounding off. But because the European Union refused to release the currency until the very last moment, everyone simply ignored it. The first of January arrived and the entire population awoke to a wallet full of bills that were about as familiar as Albanian Blotniks. In fact, the conversion had been fixed several years ago at 6.591 francs to the Euro, a number that Brussels figured would be easy to remember. As soon as the stores open after the New Year's holiday, I trot down to rue de Rivoli to enjoy the show.

As entertaining as it is to see a grown Frenchman cry, it is still a sad and pitiful experience. I am standing behind a gnarled man at the *tabac* shop as he attempts to buy a pack of Gauloises, a French cigarette that is often favourably compared to donkey excrement.

The clerk pulls down a deck of smokes. "That will be 3 Euros and 48 cents, Monsieur."

The man takes out an ancient leather change purse attached by a stout metal chain to his belt. He unzips the coin pouch and begins to poke around, his nicotine-stained fingers nervously fingering the shiny, strange coins that nestle inside. "How much is that in francs, dammit?"

The clerk, who has a ring through his nose, takes on a strangely smug air. "I am sorry Monsieur, but the law says that I can only charge you in Euros."

The man stares at the cigarettes on the counter, so near, yet so impossibly far away, and he begins to plead. "Please, just tell me how much it is."

The clerk sighs as he reaches for a calculator. He taps the keys for a moment. "That is the equivalent of 22.93668 francs."

The man emits the sound of a leaky balloon full of mud. Tears rolling down his stubbly cheeks, he pours the contents of his change purse out onto the counter. "Here, take it. Take it all." The clerk counts out the required change and hands over the cigarettes. I can't help but smile condescendingly as he shuffles off, sniffling at the prospect of a lifetime of humiliation at the hands of someone with facial metallica.

I stride forward and place my newspaper and magazines down in front of the clerk. He glances at me. "Do you want to know how much that is in francs, too, Monsieur?"

By coincidence, the Euro and the Canadian dollar are very close in value. For the first time in several months, I haven't had to go through the gymnastics of converting to my home currency. "No, that's not necessary."

Visibly disappointed, he picks up his hand–held laser and scans in my purchases. "That will be 8 Euros."

I glance at the total. "You've made an error. It's only 7 Euros."

The clerk picks through the pile and repeats my tally. Sure enough, it comes to 8 Euros. He rolls his eyes and asks me if I need any help counting out my change. I grab my goods and, as I leave, idly wonder how painful it is to have a nose ring pulled out with pliers.

Saturday morning arrives sharp and brisk. Fortunately, Maurice the plumber arrives in similar fashion, ready to tackle the job. His pockets are stuffed with a cellphone, the sports newspaper, *L'Equipe*, and, as an afterthought, numerous wrenches. On his wrist is a very expensive Rolex. He is accompanied by his apprentice, a young man with a gap-toothed grin, a set of blue coveralls labelled "Vincent," and the largest ears I have ever seen on a *Homo sapiens*. A heavy tool chest is looped over his shoulder with a thick leather strap.

The hot water heater is mounted on the wall in the bedroom closet. Maurice climbs inside and conducts an intimate examination of its nether regions before pronouncing that a heaterectomy is in order. "Fortunately, I have the perfect replacement outside." Their vehicle is a Renault side-panel truck, about the size of a picnic cooler on wheels. I watch in admiration as they extricate a huge box from the back and uncrate a brand-new cylinder. With Vincent holding the bottom, Maurice guides the heater up the spiral staircase to our apartment. Wrestling the old unit out of the closet, they soon have the new one bolted onto the wall and ready to connect. I gleefully begin to rummage through my bath salts and tub toys in anticipation.

Maurice, however, has other plans. "Just in time," he announces.

"In time for what?" I ask.

Maurice pulls out *L'Equipe*. "Why, the match, of course."

Les Bleus, France's national team, are playing in a friendly match against a Balkan nation that is so tiny that I didn't even think it had a Chinese takeaway, let alone a soccer team. Carefully storing their tools, Maurice and Vincent march out the door and down the street to the local café to watch the game. When they return several hours later, I assume either France must have been victorious, or the wine very good, because they are both in an excellent, pink-cheeked mood.

In a few short minutes, they have the final connections made and turn on the new heater. I am already grabbing for my towel when Maurice stops me. "You must wait for one day," he cautions.

"Why?"

He shoves a clipboard under my nose to sign. "Because that is how long it takes for the water to warm up."

My response is lost in the kitchen sink.

I have noticed recently that my arms are starting to resemble an orangutan's. This is not from the intake of too many bananas, but from carrying cases of wine for half a kilometre. I have come to the conclusion that I need something for transporting my wine, and although I am thinking of a Porsche, Linda suggests we check out the caddies, instead. A caddy is a small, two-wheeled personal shopping cart made of lightweight metal and canvas. BHV has a wide selection of models, and so we find ourselves heading down to the department store at probably the worst possible time of the year, the annual January sale.

Unlike in North America, where sales occur every fifteen minutes, in France stores are prohibited from lowering their prices except for two officially sanctioned sales periods—one in July and one in January. About a week before the event, retailers begin to scour the basement for all the things they couldn't sell the year before—turquoise bowling shoes, python-food blenders, and lampshades decorated with the European Union logo. They then stack them in messy piles under screaming pink signs announcing that, at prices like these, the merchandise will literally disappear from under your nose. On the fateful day, the doors are flung open and a horde of shoppers, whipped into a veritable frenzy, haul great armloads to the till where the cashiers promptly go on coffee break.

Linda and I arrive at BHV in the midst of this mayhem. For some unfathomable reason, the caddy section is almost deserted, even though several models in green polka dots and chartreuse stripes are being offered at half price. Sighing, I chose a convertible ragtop model in metallic burgundy.

The wet, damp weather that has plagued the month finally breaks on Monday, and I take advantage of the clear skies to do my morning shopping chores. Snazzy caddy in hand, I set out on foot for rue de Rivoli. Quartering south along the narrow streets, I pass Camille's, where the waiters are hunched around the bar inside, warming their hands against the coffee machine. Along rue Pavée, Hassidic Jews in long coats and black fedoras skirt around the ice that has formed on puddles the evening before. The smell of sweet chocolate pastries and croissants wafts from a bakery door.

Walking in the Marais is a vital skill in itself, a kind of balancing act between admiring the scenery and avoiding being mangled to death. The #29 bus that runs along rue des Francs-Bourgeois comes equipped with a warning device that sounds exactly like the old-fashioned bells on bicycle handlebars, only a lot louder. Delivery vans, on the other hand, assume that you will hear the roar of their engines as they try to break the world speed record for five-ton trucks.

Why not simply stick to the sidewalks? For two reasons. First, they are so narrow that it is impossible for a baby carriage and a shopping cart to pass on sidewalks. Second, they are already occupied by traffic, either of the stationary kind, as in parked cars, or the mobile kind, as in scooters.

The Marais pedestrian thus learns to adopt a technique well known to anyone dodging sniper fire—the random lateral zigzag. This manoeuvre is indispensable whenever a Fiat barges onto the sidewalk, or a piece of masonry detaches itself from a crumbling building. Grocery caddies tend to limit one's agility, however, and so I favour walking down the middle of the asphalt against traffic. This gives me sufficient scope to spot oncoming Peugeots in time to get out of their way. The main, sometimes fatal, flaw of this technique is the driver who insists on reversing down the entire length of a one-way street while talking on his cellphone and lighting a cigarette. The only defense is to keep a sharp ear peeled for the tell-tale whine of an abused transmission and leap for the nearest doorway.

When I reach rue de Rivoli, I stop to talk to Jean-Pierre. "You have a good weekend?"

"Yes!" Jean-Pierre grins happily. "Luck was with me at the horse races. And you?"

"We went to the Petit Bofinger brasserie for lunch this weekend."

"Ah! Excellent food."

"You know the restaurant?"

"I trained the chef."

I begin to wonder if Jean-Pierre has a few other bad habits. "Are you sure you haven't been drinking too much cooking wine?"

"It's true!" As proof, he shows me the twenty-years'-service watch presented to him by the owners of a nearby restaurant.

"That's a very nice timepiece."

Jean-Pierre beams. "Whenever I need a little extra cash, I pawn it."

In France, all pawnshops are run by the federal government. The main Paris outlet, located just around the corner from our house, was set up in 1777 when Louis XVI bowed to demand from the aristocracy. "People would pawn their clothes on Monday, then buy them back on Saturday to wear to church on Sunday," explains Janice, the tour guide, when I ask her several days later. "They were given half the amount that they might get at auction, and charged 1 per cent interest on the money leant. If they didn't reclaim them in one month, they were sold at auction."

"Is pawning still popular?"

"Of course. When you've pawned something, the French say it is *chez ma tante*, at my aunt's."

Whatever the exact terms, business was so brisk that the old auction room had to be abandoned in favour of a new, larger facility. Rather than gut the old space, however, the city leased it to a restaurateur who promptly established the Dome du Marais, one of the most unique eateries in the city.

Linda and I stop by for dinner in late January, just as the first lamb is coming into season. When we enter the main dining room, we are astounded. The room is one large cylinder, fifteen metres in diameter, rising to a glass dome approximately eighteen metres above. The walls are decorated with frescoes, gilt wallpaper, and ornate carvings. In the centre of the room is a trio of 3.6-metre alabaster cupids holding up a cluster of illuminated orbs. I feel as though I am in the middle of an immense jar of Christmas candies.

After an *amuse bouche* of finely minced roast pork in lard and a glass of the house *fumé blanc*, our lamb cutlets arrive in a citrus glaze accompanied by pancakes of coarsely shredded potato. For dessert, the chef prepares a medley of chocolate cake, ice cream, and hot fudge laid out in artistic style on our plates. And the best part of the meal is that we don't have to pawn anything to pay for it. The *prix fixe* is half the price we might have paid for a similar meal in London, even without the cupids. I raise a glass of Sauternes and toast Louis's *tante*.

There is a tiny coffee shop on the corner. The walls are covered with several dozen different clocks, none of which tells the correct time. It is a perfect place to relax and have a morning espresso and croissant, secure in the knowledge that you can simply tell the boss you have no idea what time it is when you roll into work late. When Ramon arrives back from a fashion photography shoot in the Maldives, I suggest we go there for a drink.

Although Ramon is tanned from his sojourn in the Indian Ocean, he isn't very relaxed. "What's wrong?" I ask.

Ramon glances around the café and sneers. "It's full of *Bobos*."

"What?"

"Bourgeois Bohemians. They are rich, but they don't want to look it, so they live in the Marais. They drop their kids off at the crèche and then come in to have a coffee and compare jewellery."

Now that he mentions it, the café *is* filled with women in frosted hair and designer sports gear pushing Louis Vuitton prams. According to Ramon, these suede-clad invaders are ruining the Marais, driving up housing costs, replacing butcher shops with earring emporiums, and parking their Range Rovers in handicapped spots normally reserved for bar owners. Just to cheer him up, I suggest we finish our coffee and go in search of doorways.

If you happen to possess an obsession for doors, then the Marais is heaven. Marais doors tend to be large, wooden, double-hinged affairs, designed to swing open wide enough to let a carriage and four horses exit with aplomb. They are tall and rounded in an arch at the top and painted in various shades of red, green, and grey. Many still have heavy iron plates bolted into the oak, put there to stall a mob with a battering ram long enough to boil a pot of oil. Now that's what I call a door.

The door at 23, rue Barbette is disappointingly small, hardly large enough to let a parson's dogcart and donkey through, but just across the street from us is a magnificent portal. The twin doors soar six metres above the pavement and are decorated with a double cameo of a beautiful young woman. The archway, in solid limestone, has been carved with a curious coral relief, and if you look closely enough at the lintel, you can make out the ghostly imprint of the former address, rue des Clouteries.

Ramon's favourite doorway is a large red affair on rue Vieille du Temple, just south of rue de Bretagne. It is so big that a special, smaller door has been cut in the middle for pedestrians to enter. If you stand across the street and consume some hallucinogens, you will notice that the trim on the door has been designed to resemble the stylized helmet of a medieval knight.

My favourite door is just down the street at 47, rue Vieille du Temple. The entrance to the Hôtel Amelot de Bisseuil features a twin set of garish Medusa heads in bas relief. This is not a door for shy Fuller Brush salesmen—the matching visage is twisted into an evil grin, and the snakes upon Medusa's head writhe in suitably hideous fashion. The protective varnish has long since worn off, and the wood is cracked and dirty, but this just adds to the effect. The site originally belonged to the Marshal of Rieux, a companion-in-arms to Joan of Arc. When the hotel was rebuilt in the seventeenth century, the owners opted for the grisly adornment. Their choice of decorations has had a lasting impact on passing pedestrians. Although the walls of the street are smeared with spray-paint graffiti, nobody has ever so much as run a penknife across Medusa's visage.

When we arrive at the gorgons, we are delighted to see

that the portal is ajar, so we sneak inside. A large van sits in the courtyard, and movers in blue work coats are carrying household goods down a wide staircase. The furniture is in the style of Louis XVI, but these aren't reproductions—the finish on the marble-topped sideboards, gilt mirrors, and ornate tables is clouded with age.

I am pleasantly surprised to discover there are two courtyards connected by a short passageway. The courtyard walls are clad in a warm, honey-coloured limestone and feature several large sundials decorated with numerous insignia, their paint faded by the centuries to almost nothing. Numerous busts and statues occupy niches carved in the walls, and a travertine horse trough rests inside the short passageway. We are about to investigate further when a stony-faced doorman appears and tells us in no uncertain terms that we are trespassing. We beat a hasty retreat and go our separate ways, me heading east on rue des Francs-Bourgeois in search of a place to enjoy the feeble sunshine.

There are scores of courtyards throughout the Marais, quiet oases reached by a long passageway, but few are available to the law-abiding public. The Hôtel Carnavalet, just off rue des Francs-Bourgeois on rue de Sévigné, is an exception. Now the official city museum, it not only chronicles the history of Paris from Neolithic times to the French Revolution, but it also possesses a magnificent enclosed garden.

During the seventeenth century, the Hôtel Carnavalet was home to one of France's most celebrated women of letters, Madame de Sévigné. A gifted writer, she was widowed at the age of twenty-three when her husband was shot in a duel over another man's wife. Over the next several decades, she chronicled Marais court life in letters to her friends and children, detailing how the brother of Louis XIV liked to dress up in ladies' clothing, or telling the tale of the cook who committed suicide when the fish arrived too late for a dinner the king was attending.

I stop in at the museum shop and pick up a pamphlet detailing the life of the former tenant and tales of the Marais before planting myself on a garden bench in the sunshine. I sit alone, my breath rising in a cloud of vapour. Even in the dead of winter, the garden still possesses a somber charm, isolated from the bustle of rue des Francs-Bourgeois, solemn and regal.

I open the pamphlet and read about Madame Brinvilliers, one of France's most prolific poisoners. Married to an uncaring military officer, she took up with a lover named Godin, but her father had him imprisoned in the Bastille. There, a fellow prisoner sold him his poison secrets—toad spit, arsenic, and antimony—and when he got out, Godin shared them with his mistress. First, she poisoned her father, then her two brothers, and then she tried to poison her husband. Godin, fearing he might be next, gave the husband the antidote.

Suspicions were raised, but investigators were stymied by the lack of proof. According to contemporary law, the only way the authorities could prosecute was to find the original poison and test it out on a dog. Eventually, Godin died unexpectedly, and when incriminating evidence was found, the Madame was put on trial. Found guilty in 1676, she was tortured and decapitated, and her remains were burnt at the stake.

I fold up the pamphlet and rise from the bench. There's nothing like a little sunshine on a cold January day to lift the spirits.

"See here? That's where they broke in." Nigel and I are standing in the basement of 23, rue Barbette. My upstairs neighbour is pointing to a hole in a brick wall, now patched up, through which thieves had gained entrance to his wine cellar. "They stole 18,000 francs worth of wine. When the insurance man came, he looked at the receipts and said 'But you had it four years—it wouldn't be worth as much.'" Nigel laughs in derision. "Hah! The nerve."

I had wanted to see if there was any spare room in the basement for storage, and Nigel volunteered to give me a tour. Entrance to the cellar is through a door off the foyer, down a circular stone staircase. A series of low barrel vaults have been constructed of thick blocks of roughly-hewn limestone. The walls are covered with great patches of black lichen, no doubt the ancestral grounds to the colony that infests my shower stall. The entire basement has an aroma that, were it an automobile air freshener, would come in the shape of the Bastille. I peer into the gloom, idly searching for the man in the iron mask.

I had already learned that every square centimetre of soil in Paris has a story, but until our tour of the basement, I had never before wondered about my own home. I ask Nigel if he knows much about the history of the building, but he simply shrugs his shoulders and slaps one of the thick stone walls. "Built to last, that's all I know."

I am out on rue des Francs-Bourgeois a few days later when I once again pass the sign marking the spot where, in 1407, the Duke of Burgundy had his cousin, the Duke of Orleans, murdered, "assassinated while the latter was visiting Queen Isabeau at the Hôtel Barbette." Was this, I wondered, the origin of the name of our street? Was I living on the same spot as one of France's most notorious rulers?

I head down to the Paris Historical Society on rue François Miron, near the Hôtel de Ville, and ask for their help in researching the address. The volunteer librarian pulls out several tomes and I am soon lost in a pile of historical ephemera. Maps from the thirteenth century show that the Marais was originally home to several monasteries, some of which featured flagellation, in which acolytes beat one another with stout wooden staffs (today, of course, this practice is confined to the hockey rink). According to the maps, the land under rue Barbette belonged to the convent of Sainte-Catherine.

The Barbettes were an affluent family of Parisian bankers, and several of them served as merchant provosts to the king. Sometime around the thirteenth century, the family took over control of a large portion of the convent fields and established a walled compound. The family domain grew in style and grandeur over the next century, with orchards and fancy homes appearing within the walls. During the early 1300s, however, the Barbettes were implicated in Philippe le Bon's surreptitious attempts to add lead to the silver coinage. When the local population took umbrage, the king fled to the safety of the Knights Templar's castle down the road, and the mobs had to settle for pillaging the Barbette's compound. Ah, there's nothing like seeing a banker's home being burned to the ground to warm a Parisian's heart.

Over the next hundred years, the Barbettes subdivided part of their land and sold it to weavers and drapers. There was still a sufficiently large portion remaining for Nicolas de Mauregard, treasurer of France, to build the second Hôtel Barbette in 1390, which was subsequently purchased by Charles VI and given to his wife, Isabeau of Bavaria.

Isabeau was a beautiful, sensuous woman who used the hotel as her getaway spot, especially when Charles fell into one of his periodic fits of madness. Louis, Duke of Orleans and the king's brother, was handsome, ambitious, and immoral, and

Isabeau invited him to become her intimate companion at the well-guarded mansion, a fact that the queen took few pains to conceal.

On the other hand, Jean, Duke of Burgundy, was small, quarrelsome, and tight-fisted. Not only did he hate Louis for thwarting his plans to rule the government, he was also jealous of his own wife's weakness for the handsome man. The cunning duke plotted to take advantage of Louis's notoriously scandalous behaviour with the queen.

On the night of 23 November 1407, Louis was summoned from supper at the Hôtel Barbette by an "urgent message from the king." As he left the main entrance, assassins knocked him to the ground and split his skull with an ax. The citizens of the city were appalled by the attack against the popular Orleans, and Burgundy was forced to flee ahead of the angry mobs.

Isabeau abandoned Hôtel Barbette, and the land passed through various hands until the mid-1500s, when it was bought by developers. The remains of the mansion were knocked down and the land subdivided. Taking a cue from its royal lineage, the newly christened rue Barbette came into existence in 1563, and various mansions soon followed.

I carefully scan the city maps for the seventeenth century. A building at 23, rue Barbette first appears in the mid-1600s, when various homes were constructed on the north side of the street. The original building was a portal structure facing the road, with a double door leading to the inner garden. The developers followed traditional building methods used since the Middle Ages. The basement was constructed using a series of barrel vaults made of sandstone blocks. Then carpenters installed a massive frame of thirty-centimetre-thick oak lumber extending all the way up to the roof. Smaller beams were strung across to create support for flooring, and the roof was finished off in slate tiles. The walls were then filled in with a combination of smaller joists and mortar. Fireplaces and chimneys were installed, and the interior walls finished with lathe and plaster. Double circular stairways made of iron, one on each side of the foyer, were put in place.

The first residents of note, the brothers Massu, shared the royal apartment floor, with its high ceilings and regal trappings. As tax collectors under Louis XVI, they could afford to expand the apartment, and the two wings built onto the back of the building may have dated from this period. The French revolution ended the Massu family's occupation (and probably the Massus). When the Terror finally abated, the apartment was taken over by the Comtesse de Failly of Luxembourg, until 1834.

By this time, the Marais had definitely fallen from fashion, and the apartment was subdivided and sold off to various families. On the *étage noble*, the mouldings and fireplace were torn out, and huge optical grinding machines were lifted through the front windows and installed.

The building was saved from the wrecker's ball in the mid-1960s, when André Malraux, the minister of culture, decreed the Marais a national treasure and set aside funds for its rejuvenation. In the early 1980s, developers bought up 23, rue Barbette and gave it new life. The horse stables on the main floor became a photographer's studio. The factory equipment was also discarded, and the upper floors upgraded to modern residential standards.

Only the basement remains the same. I rise from my research and descend the circular staircase to stand in the dimness. I place my hand on the cool stone wall, and the surface crumbles beneath my palm. I feel the weight of the centuries upon it and am filled with an overwhelming thought: maybe I'll come down later tonight and take a crack at Nigel's wine cellar.

FÉVRIER

Living in Paris has one tremendous benefit: you do not need a car. In fact, it is preferable not to own one. Not only is gasoline more expensive and less tasty than malt whiskey, it is also easier to remove your own kidney stones with a pencil than it is to find a legal parking spot. The viable alternative is public transit, which is clean, safe, and punctual. You can get anywhere in town in half the time and twice the comfort. In short, you'd have to be insane to own a car.

Anyway, that's the rationalization. As a North American, I believe it is my God-given right to raise the temperature of the Antarctic by driving to the end of the block in an SUV the size of Saskatchewan every time I need a bag of shrimp-flavoured potato chips.

I miss my car. And that's not all. I miss home delivery, too. The French think they're civilized when it comes to food, but unless you want a pizza that makes your dog's Frisbee taste good, forget it. And don't get me started on the state of radio in this country. There are at least twenty FM stations in the Paris area, and each one features a continual broadcast of everything from rap to classic. Not an hour goes by without being serenaded by a Bach concerto, only to be followed by a charming melody tentatively titled "Screw You Sideways with a Crowbar, Mutha."

The only thing worse than radio here is TV. Contrary to what I imagined, about one third of all shows on French TV are American programming, with everything from *South Park* to *Friends* being shown on a nightly basis. And if you don't think that can get any worse, they dub the soundtrack into French. In addition to the queasy feeling you get watching Calista Flockhart's lips fly about her face hopelessly out of sync, there is something distinctly creepy about hearing a stranger's voice coming out of her head.

Something is wrong. I no longer love Paris. The days are short, wet, and windy, and the nights long, cold, and dark. Even on nice days, it is all I can do to force myself out the door.

It seems that the whole town feels the same way. Dragging myself reluctantly out of our apartment, I head down to the butcher's on rue de Bretagne to buy some chops for our evening meal. To my consternation, a palpable cloud of disquiet hangs over the shop. Between Monsieur and Madame Savoy, there moves a glacier of unspoken accusations and denials. I am, of course, immediately intrigued, and wonder what juicy details are being concealed beneath their mute standoff. Did the Monsieur wink once too often at the slim, pretty blonde who comes in once a week to purchase a roast and always leaves with a hand-tied packet of tidbits for her toy poodle? Had the Madame stuffed too much paprika into the chorizo, inducing a crescendo of complaints from the customers?

After buying my chops, I go next door to the wine store, where Natalie is busy pounding with great vigour at something in the window.

"A new display?"

"No, cockroaches." Natalie nails one more with a satisfying crunch before clambering out.

"Natalie, have you noticed how depressed people are lately?" Natalie pats her red curls back into place. "But of course. People get tired of all the rain and dark. They throw themselves under a Metro train or off the roof."

Thus cheered, I wheel my caddy back down rue Vieille du Temple, keeping a careful eye peeled for plummeting Frenchmen. Fortunately, it is a relatively quiet day for jumpers, and I reach home unscathed. I decide the best course of action is to go back to bed. While scanning the newspaper, I read a lifestyle article about North Americans living abroad. It outlines a progression of commonly experienced perceptions: from the initial infatuation with their new home, to disenchantment when they realize that day-to-day living is just as hard, if not harder, than in their home environment, to a feeling of frustration, insecurity, and lack of confidence that leads to withdrawal, dementia, and one-way trips under the Metro. Well, that about sums it up—I am suffering from "expat fever," a combination of homesickness, mental constipation, and rampant cultural phobia. I pull the covers up over my head and have a good weep.

Like all fine soulmates, Linda is sympathetic to my plight and offers a decisive course of action. "Either straighten up, or I'll toss you out the window."

Predictably, that focuses my mind. I know that I have to do something, and fast. Should I go on a holiday, telephone friends back home, or, as an absolute last resort, learn to speak French? Hey, I may be demented, but I'm not crazy.

I decide to buy a DVD player. This, I reason, would allow

me to rent all the latest un-dubbed movies from Hollywood. Through the miracle of modern electronics, I could once again get my fix of spectacular car crashes, burning buildings, and gunfights in their original language. On a blustery February morning, I make my way down to BHV. The department store is featuring a "special sale," not to be confused with the official sale, which was over in January. Not only are they offering a veritable pantheon of brand names, but also their prices are so unbelievably low that you'd be a fool not to buy two of everything.

I had been warned that DVD manufacturers had created different functionality zones to prevent movie piracy. Discs sold in Europe, for instance, would not work in North American DVD players, and vice versa. When I finally find a sales clerk who isn't on coffee break, I ask to see a DVD player that isn't too criminally expensive, but still allows me to play all zones. Rubbing a nasty boil on the back of his neck, he directs me to a model I have never heard of, but he assures me that it is easy to convert to universal play—I just have to follow the English section of my instruction manual. Like a lobster hopping into the pot to see if the water is warm enough, I obligingly buy the DVD player.

The first harbinger of woe occurs when I discover the instruction manual is in French, German, Spanish, and Latvian only. Like all men, I ignore instruction manuals until I have spent at least two hours in a futile attempt trying to patch the DVD onto my TV. According to the French and Latvian sections of the manual, the cable supplied by the manufacturer is only for use in connecting the DVD to the space shuttle. Toasters, TVs, and other mundane objects require a special cable.

I return to BHV to search out the salesman. I find him hiding beneath a stereo display and explain the problem. Slapping his forehead in astonishment, he leads me over to another display where, for a mere 40 Euros, I can buy the correct cable that would absolutely, without a doubt in the world, work this time.

I finally connect my DVD, pop in a disc, and order up the menu. Following the instructions, I program my language of choice to Urdu, or what I assumed to be Urdu, since I don't even recognize the alphabet. After much more fumbling, I finally manage to start the movie, only to discover a large red patch in the middle of Brad Pitt's face. Since I hadn't noticed any unsightly blemishes on his visage before, I assume it might be a malfunctioning disc and take it back to the rental shop.

The clerk, a charming young woman named Laurence, is very sympathetic. Listening to my explanation, she patiently pops the offending disc into the store DVD, which promptly plays the movie without any problems at all. She helpfully suggests I either adjust my medication or take the DVD player back.

Returning merchandise in France is like performing home dentistry on a cat, only more painful. Most department stores hire women with large, bulging forearms and short hair to man the returns desk. Their policy is, "you bought it, you own it," and the only way they are taking it back is if you mud wrestle them first.

Cowardice is also the lowest form of wisdom, so I decide instead to take it to the repairs department. Auspiciously, the clerk is an elderly, balding man with a permanent stoop. I march confidently up to the desk, firmly place my appliance down, and adopt my most authoritative voice. "There's something terribly wrong with my DVD player."

The clerk peers at me over his bifocals with a look of

amazement. "We've never had a problem with any of our DVD players before, Monsieur. Are you sure you bought it here?" To his obvious disappointment, I produce the relevant documentation. After writing down my long list of complaints, he reluctantly carries it off to the back.

"How long will it take to fix?" I shout after him.

The clerk's reply is a metaphysical shrug. "Who knows anything for certain, Monsieur?"

I go home and stare at my TV, silently weeping every time Frasier utters "*sacre bleu!*" Would I ever see my DVD player again?

Much to my surprise, I receive a postcard two weeks later announcing that my DVD player is ready for pickup. Hurrying down, I present my receipt to the same clerk, who disappears for a half-hour smoke before triumphantly returning with my appliance.

"What was wrong?" I ask.

The clerk peels off the technician's report and scans down the list. "Nothing. They recommend you read the manual."

I carry the DVD player back home and plug it in, my heart weary with the weight of defeat. When the movie comes on, however, I am delighted to discover Brad Pitt's red complexion has been miraculously cured. It's amazing what they can do with hormone cream these days.

Linda decides that a little diversion would be the best remedy for my winter blues, and what better diversion than the upcoming St. Valentine's Day? As you might expect, the French hold the holiday in high regard. Taking me firmly in hand, we head for Printemps.

Located near the Opera House, Printemps is one of

the premier department stores in Paris, catering to lovers of everything chic. In fact, the entire basement floor is devoted to just one thing—lady's lingerie. Descending by escalator, we are greeted by my version of heaven: an endless display of lavender thongs and black bustiers dotted with tiny roses.

Not only do the French have the world's best lingerie shops, but they also allow another innovation that ranks right up there with the quick-release brassiere: unisex change rooms. Actually, unisex might be the incorrect term—there aren't many man-size frillies in stock—but they *do* allow boyfriends behind the curtains to inspect their sweethearts in all their glory. Together, we pick out a lovely red silk camisole-and-pant-set.

As the big day approaches, I plan out the meal. First, a bottle of Heidsieck Blue Top Brut champagne and some smoked salmon for the *amuse bouche*. Next, a box of chocolate-dipped cherries from the neighbourhood *chocolaterie* for dessert. Finally, a delightful Saint-Emilion Bordeaux red to go with the meal.

I can't decide what main course to cook, however. Since my last disquieting visit, I had been avoiding the butcher on rue de Bretagne. Instead, I'd been making do with whatever I could find in the meat counter at Monoprix supermarket. But this was Valentine's Day—a slab of calf's liver in onions simply isn't, well, romantic.

I am pondering my plight when I pass a rotisserie on rue Saint-Antoine, near the Saint-Paul Metro station. A large, cheerful assistant butcher with very crooked teeth stands out front with a client, an elderly woman in red, patent-leather shoes. He points to each cooked bird, asking her if she would like to invite *Amélie*, or perhaps *Rosalie*, for dinner.

I glance inside. The shop is crammed with a wide variety

of poultry, pork, beef, and lamb, the certificates of authenticity prominently displayed. Monsieur Fontaine, the *artisan boucher*, stands behind the counter. A small man with a pencil mustache, he wears his white apron with one strap off the shoulder, not so much out of fashion sense but because the strap is broken. I step into line with all the other customers.

When my turn arrives, Fontaine asks me my pleasure. I gaze at all the carefully prepared meats, unsure of what to pick. He leans over the counter and helpfully points to a selection in the poultry section. "Have you ever tried a *pintade farcie?*"

Pintade farcie turns out to be wild fowl stuffed with a mixture of minced veal, mushrooms, spices, and breadcrumbs. Fontaine had first removed the breast and carcass bones, then filled the cavity with the *farcie* and trussed it back up, creating a boneless stuffed bird. I gladly purchase the concoction and take it home to roast.

That night, as a winter storm rages outside, we bask in the glow of candlelight. The slices of *pintade*, served with gravy prepared from the drippings, go very well with the Bordeaux. It is a lovely, romantic evening, and, best of all, we inaugurate Linda's new lingerie in the name of St. Valentine.

Encouraged by her success at getting me out of my shell, Linda announces that, from now on, we will get out of the house at least once a week to see a movie.

The French love cinema, and the city is dotted with several hundred theatres dedicated to the silver screen. They range from the very humble to grand multiplexes with plush seats, immense screens, and multi-channel stereo systems.

The French cinema experience is subtly different from the North American variety. First of all, the French serve two types of popcorn: sweet and salty. The sweet version is similar to caramel corn, only the glaze is a simple spray of white sugar. The second variety is seasoned with a blend of hand-gathered sea salt that has been sun-dried in Brittany. Both are about as popular as a worm sandwich and are invariably so stale that you have to pre-soak them in diet Coke or risk fracturing a molar.

Every show begins with about thirty minutes of ads. Most are prepared especially for the big screen, however, and are far more entertaining than their TV counterparts. One of my favourites involves a businessman returning home in the evening. As he advances up the walk to his apartment block, he steps in a pile of fresh dog shit. When he arrives at the front door of an apartment inside, he wipes his feet vigorously on the welcome mat and then, instead of opening the door, he continues down the hall to his own home. I have no idea what they are advertising, but the entire audience howls in pure delight whenever they see it.

We once attended a French-made movie. Most of the film consisted of a series of very depressed people talking endlessly in cafés about their neuroses or sleeping with their best friend's spouse. The only way we knew it was over was when the lights came up and the audience left.

Fortunately, Hollywood movies are quite popular. Many Parisian moviegoers prefer to see them in their original version with the dialogue subtitled in French. This is especially true of any movie by Woody Allen, who the French consider a minor, balding deity. But then, they also love Jerry Lewis. Go figure.

No trip to the cinema in Paris is complete without going out for dinner afterward. After catching the latest Michael Douglas film at the Odeon Cinema in Saint-Germain des

Prés, we decide to take advantage of a rainless evening to walk over to the Latin Quarter. Situated on the Left Bank across from Notre-Dame, the quarter is the original site of the Roman town built by Caesar. It is a twisting maze of cobblestone lanes with such names as "the alleyway of the cat who fishes," and the buildings tend to lean drunkenly against one another like stag partiers coming out of a pub. Although the area was an informal dormitory for university students during the Middle Ages, it is now completely filled with tourist hotels and tiny Greek restaurants. Large platters of raw lamb, pork, and salmon, arranged onto long steel skewers and ready for the grill, crowd the display windows.

One of the restaurants, the Dionysus, features a large pig roasting on a spit, and we decide to eat there. Once inside, we realize that the spit in the window is actually in the front part of the kitchen, with the rest of the kitchen arranged along one wall of the main dining room. Behind the counter stands a tall Algerian man wearing a white chef's hat. Although it is not immediately apparent, he is just entering the stage of withdrawal where his medication no longer controls the violent outbursts of temper that twenty years of peeling onions and chopping carrots has induced.

We sit down and decide to have some pork from the spit. When told of our order by the waiter, the chef demurs, pointing out that it isn't done yet. The waiter replies that he can see with his own two eyes that the pig is perfectly cooked, and that the chef should do as he is told, or he will be sent back to Algiers where the local *imam*s might not be so charitable to someone who makes a living carving up unclean animals.

The chef responds by picking up a very large cleaver. "You want pork?" he shouts, swinging the cleaver violently at the spit. "I'll give you pork!" Chunks of seared flesh begin careening through the air in an alarming fashion, and we are trying to decide if flight might be better than an appetizer when something remarkable happens. A tourist from Alabama, dressed in white pants and a baseball cap, announces to his wife Martha that the folks back home just won't believe it if he "don't get a picture." Taking out his digital video camera, he stands up and approaches the kitchen counter. Having never seen someone's head cleft in two before, let alone a JVC, we decide to stay and observe the festivities.

Starting up his camera, the man positions himself right behind the chef, who by this time is busily immersing his un-cleavered hand into a pile of tomato and lettuce garnish and flinging it in ungarnished directions. The moment the light from the camera comes on, however, he turns abruptly.

It is a magnificent cinematic tableau: the chef, a grease-smeared cleaver in one hand, a fistful of salad in the other, confronted by the cyclopean digital eye of a used car salesman from Mobile. My most earnest wish is that he has taken the cap off the lens. He is sure to win first prize on TV's "*Famous Last Bloopers*" show.

Astonishingly, the sight of the camera has a calming effect on the chef. He puts down the cleaver and straightens his cap, all the while smiling shyly at the lens. No amount of coaxing, including a financial incentive, can entice him to take up the cleaver and make even a feeble whack at the pig. In the end, much to our chagrin, the American is left with footage of an Algerian grinning sheepishly in front of a mutilated roast instead of the much more interesting shot of his fingers rolling around on the kitchen counter like pink sausages. A typical French ending.

They are performing Mozart at Sainte-Chapelle tonight. The thirteenth-century church, built by Saint-Louis, has to be one of my favourite buildings in the world. Nestled into the court-yard of the Palais de Justice on the Ile de la Cité, the church is appealing not only for its architectural splendour, but also for its story. In 1239, Beaudoin, Emperor of Constantinople, needed money for a military venture and hocked the crown to the Venetians. When he couldn't repay the debt, the Venetians contacted the king of France. Louis knew a celestial bargain when he saw one and redeemed the crown, along with a few handy sacred nails and slivers of wood that had been thrown in to sweeten the bargain. Naturally, Louis needed a suitable space to house the holy relics and he commissioned Pierre of Montreuil to build a chapel, which the architect built in a mere three years, the exterior walls being composed solely of stained glass and delicate, almost ethereal, stone columns.

The effect is truly amazing. Sitting in the main chapel, my eyes follow colourful biblical scenes as they ascend the walls to the immense roof, which is painted blue and covered with gold fleurs-de-lys that sparkle like stars in the night sky. The notes from the string quartet float through the air and fill this magical place with perfect music, no doubt pleasing the spirits of Jesus, Saint-Louis, and Mozart.

Curiously, the earthly whereabouts of all three men share a similar dispersal. Christ, of course, got up and left the tomb for points celestial under his own steam. The remnants of Saint-Louis were exhumed from their resting spot in Saint-Denis during the Revolution and scattered to the four winds. And Mozart, who ended up in a pauper's grave, had his bones dispersed by scavenging dogs. May they all rest peacefully tonight in Sainte-Chapelle.

I am frantic. The Winter Olympics are taking place in Salt Lake City, and Canada and the United States are in the hockey finals. The Canadians haven't won Olympic gold in fifty years and the Americans never lost it with home ice advantage. With both teams packed with top NHL players, it promises to be a big-hitting, wide open game.

The only problem is finding somewhere to watch it in France. Except for the downhill skiing and figure skating events, the Winter Olympics have to compete with the women's professional weightlifting finals in Calais for space on French TV. Coverage of hockey is minimal unless it's a game between France and Greece, in which case I'd just as soon watch the women's weightlifting.

Fortunately, the Moose has come to the rescue. Mark has commandeered a telecom satellite and bootlegged the feed from the BBC, which has decided to carry the final (complete with their own announcers), on their specialty sports channel.

I head down early to ensure a place to sit. At least two hundred people are already jammed in, and it is only through Mark's intercession that I am able to get a stool at the bar. Mark had called in all available staff, including Sheila, an Australian barmaid with the genial attitude of a puff adder. I order up a few jugs of draft from Sheila and wait for the show to begin.

By 9 PM, there are over three hundred people packed into the bar, mostly Canadians, with a few game Yanks thrown in. A lusty cheer arises when the puck is dropped. Even with the sound turned up full, you can barely hear the announcers, which isn't an altogether bad thing.

"The net tender demonstrated admirable flexibility."

"Yes, and that defensive man made a most valiant sacrifice, blocking the shot with his padded knees."

The Americans score first and the Yanks go nuts, but their elation is short lived as Mario Lemieux fakes the American goalie out of his shorts and sets up the tying goal.

For the next two periods, the momentum of the game swings back and forth, Canada moving ahead, then the United States catching up. Patrons in the bar, frozen into their places by the sheer numbers of people around them, chain-smoke cigarettes and guzzle down Moosehead ale. It isn't until the third period, with the frantic American team pounding shot after shot against the Canadian goalie, that that Canucks take advantage of a defensive lapse at the opposite end and move ahead. The pub breaks into a rousing chorus of "O Canada" when the final whistle blows, everyone hugging and laughing as the Canadian team spills out onto the ice to celebrate their first Olympic gold in half a century.

Shortly after, I stagger out into the street with the rest of the crowd, our clothes steaming with sweat as we step into the cool air. The local Parisians wisely head in the opposite direction, entirely unaware of the reason for so many shiny, beaming faces.

Linda, Jim, and I are bemoaning the fact that we have yet to go to a "star" restaurant. The star system was invented by the *Guide Michelin*, which rates restaurants throughout France on quality of food, service, and surroundings. Since it is Linda's birthday at the end of February, we decide to celebrate with a Saturday lunch at a two-star establishment.

La Tour d'Argent is an epicurean landmark in Paris, not only because it dates back to 1582, but also because of its dining innovations, such as the fork. A doorman dressed in a black morning coat and tie meets us at the entrance. He escorts us past a wall of photographs that includes every famous person who has ever eaten here except Adolph Hitler. We step into a small elevator and are whisked up to the top of the building, some thirty metres above the banks of the Seine.

The dining room, comfortably appointed to seat about one hundred guests, has a magnificent view. To the immediate west is Notre-Dame, while Montmartre gleams in the distance. The Marais, to the north, is obscured by apartments on Ile Saint-Louis. The room itself is decorated in conservative, functional style. The burgundy carpet boasts a gold, laurel-leaf print, and the cane-backed chairs are upholstered in olive velvet. Each table is covered with a butter-coloured cloth and a Murano duck figurine.

Behind me, against the wall, is the station used for creating the Tour's specialty, pressed duck. After the legs, wings, and breasts have been removed, the carcass is placed in a silver-plated hand press and the juice squeezed out of the remaining meat and bones. This *jus* is then strained into a flat pan and reduced. Finally, champagne and Madeira are added to create a glaze that is poured over the grilled duck.

From the moment we sit down, we are surrounded by a corps of waiters in black tuxedos. One man places the silver flatware around the table while another distributes plates and appetizers. A sommelier appears with a seven-centimetre book listing the five thousand wines stored in their cellar. After glancing at the Burgundy wine list, which includes a 1990 Romanée-Conti for 10,000 Euros, we settle on a 1994 Médoc.

While the sommelier goes off to the cellar to fetch the wine, the headwaiter comes to take our order. Although dinner at the Tour can run over 200 Euros per person, they have a set lunch for 60 Euros. We opt for the latter, ordering a starter, main, and dessert course.

While we wait for our entrées, the sommelier returns carrying our wine in a special wicker basket designed to keep the lees from rising to the top. He sets up a small side table and uncorks the wine, then slowly pours it into a decanter, using a candle to watch for any wayward lees.

For starters, Jim and Linda order duck and seafood pâtés respectively, while I have the white asparagus. The asparagus tips have been lightly steamed and are served sandwiched in puff pastry, drizzled with a butter and lemon glaze. For the main course, Jim orders medallions of lamb, whereas Linda and I opt for the duck à l'orange. The breast and thigh of the duck have been slowly grilled to rosy tenderness, and are served on a plate with the champagne and Madeira reduction. The meal is accompanied by a puff pastry filled with spinach purée. For dessert, Jim and I have multi-layered concoctions of fresh strawberries and sweet pastry, while Linda enjoys kiwi fruit, raspberries, and star fruit piled on a sponge cake soaked in mango sauce.

Just as we are finishing our meal, the proprietor comes to greet us at our table. Claude Terrail is a tall, dignified eighty-year-old who favours a green jacket and blue bachelor buttons in his lapel. He asks our names and enquires if the meal has been to our satisfaction. "It was perfect," we reply.

After lunch, we go for a walk along the Seine. It is a beautiful, sunny afternoon, with the bright towers of Notre-Dame reflecting in the choppy water. We stop to say hello to Monique, the painter, and then continue across the bridge to the place Jean XXIII. The flowerbeds have recently been dug up in preparation for planting, and a warm, earthy smell hangs in the air. Even the plane trees are beginning to show the first tinge of green beneath their brown winter bark. The feeling of isolation and blues that I had experienced just weeks ago has already lifted. Spring, I conclude, is just around the corner.

MARS

March is ushered in by a heinous North Sea storm. Boats sink in the English Channel, Breton rivers burst their banks, and the ancient chestnut trees that surround Versailles are uprooted and hurled to the ground in great, messy gnarls.

But the average Parisian couldn't care less, for spring is definitely on the way. It hangs in the air among the few brave souls who sit outside the cafés sipping their espresso and battling the wind as it shreds their newspapers. It's in the face of the young woman who rides her bicycle along rue de Rivoli, her coat open and skirt flying. It's in the crocuses that poke cheekily up through well-kept park lawns and point their yellow faces toward the pale sun.

And, as surely as winter turns to spring, so do young lovers' minds turn to marriage. John and his fiancée, Helen, decide, in a hopelessly romantic moment, to wed in Paris. Since the only person in the city who speaks French worse than I do is John, he has enlisted my help in negotiating the pitfalls of nuptial bureaucracy.

Most Paris marriages are performed at the *salle de mariage*, located in the *hôtels de ville* of the various arrondissements. The Marais city hall is a four-storey sandstone edifice built in 1867 by Napoleon III. Twin steel gates, painted blue, guard the laneway that leads through the building to the central courtyard.

A side door in the courtyard leads up to the second floor where the *salle de mariage* is located. John and I peek in. It is about fifteen metres long and seven metres wide, and the walls are decorated with faux columns painted blue, gold, and white. The ceiling, which towers nine metres above the parquet floor, is embellished with a somewhat vivid fresco of muscular nude Greeks passionately wrestling each other. John decides it is perfect.

The marriage clerk's office is located adjacent to the hall. When we ring the bell at the front counter, a young woman emerges from the bowels of a maze of cubicles. I boldly announced in French that John wants to *marrer*, and ask for the proper wedding forms. This causes two problems, as *marrer* means to have a good laugh, and the woman immediately assumes that John and I have come in to kid her about getting hitched up in a fashion that the Greek nudes next door might appreciate. We spend the next several minutes trying to convince her that an actual woman is involved, something she finds hard to believe.

Eventually, however, we straighten everything out, and the clerk produces a list of necessary documents. John scans the list, puzzled. In addition to birth certificates, blood tests, and passports, there are at least a dozen other requirements. "What's this document for?"

The clerk arches her neck to read upside down. "You need to fill that out to attest that you are single."

"And this one?"

"It is a declaration that you are not married to someone else."

"But this one already says I'm single."

"*Bais, oui.* But *this one* says that you are not married to someone else." She smiles, as if it is all perfectly clear.

Dubious, John scratches his head. "How much time will it take me to get this all together?"

The clerk thinks for a moment. "Not long. If everything goes well, eleven weeks."

"Eleven weeks! It's going to take me that long just to get married in your hall?"

"Oh, no sir. You cannot get married in our hall at all."

"Why not?"

"Because you do not live in our arrondissement. You must get married in your own arrondissement." With that, she gathers up the forms and disappears back into her cubbyhole.

That's the nice thing about French bureaucracy; you don't have to do anything particularly momentous to suffer its dead weight personally. About a week after my disastrous efforts to help John, I get a drubbing in the hands of officialdom that would do a professional wrestler proud. I had just completed writing a spy thriller and was very pleased with my opus, so thrilled, in fact, that I naively hoped that a literary agent might feel similarly disposed. Since I didn't know any literary agents personally, or even tangentially, I consulted an internet site that advised me to prepare a "submissions package." In addition to an introductory letter and sample chapters, it recommended I also include a self-addressed stamped envelope, or SASE.

One problem arises immediately; I need to purchase international postage coupons, and the phrase is not in my handy-dandy translation dictionary. I set off for *La Poste* anyway, thinking how difficult could it possibly be to explain what I want?

I arrive to discover that there is a *manifestation*, a form of work-to-rule, and there is only one clerk manning the tills. His job is to personally demonstrate how badly the general public would suffer if the government even *thought* about giving union members the old heave-ho. I spend the next twenty minutes contemplating a display case selling T-shirts with the *La Poste* logo, a delightful idea for anyone on your gift list whom you'd like to see beaten up.

I finally reach the head of the line and advance to the till, my request carefully planned out in French. "*Bonjour.* I'd like to buy an international reply stamp."

The clerk, bless his heart, actually smiles. "And what country do you want to mail it to, Monsieur?"

"England."

"Ah, England. Tell me, what is the difference between an English *frite* and a fried worm?"

I scratched my head. "I don't know."

"I thought not. Now, tell me, how many international stamps do you want?"

The clerk has drawn out a page of sixty-seven-cent stamps, the ones normally used for sending letters to the United Kingdom. "No," I respond, holding up my self-addressed envelope. "I want to buy a stamp that they can put on the envelope in the UK and mail it back here."

"Ah. So you want an envelope." The clerk disappears for several minutes into a back office before returning with a stack of envelopes. "We have an envelope with the stamp on it already. You would like these, yes?"

"Can they mail that from the UK?"

The clerk blinks his eyes once, as he suddenly realizes he is talking to the village idiot. He shakes his head and speaks slowly. "Of course not. It is good only for France."

"But I want a stamp that is good in all countries."

A woman standing in line behind me decides it is time to join the conversation. Stepping forward, she takes my self-addressed envelope and holds it under the nose of the clerk, explaining in great detail what I am looking for.

"Ah! You want a *coupon international*!

"Yes! That is what I want, a *coupon international*!"

We all beam in triumph and the clerk closes his stamp till. "I am sorry, Monsieur, but we do not have any today. Next."

There is a tramp named Giles who sits outside the Franprix grocery store near Saint-Paul Metro station. He is not a well-kept, charming panhandler like Jean-Pierre. Giles is a nasty piece of goods. Generally, he shows up around 11 AM and plops down on a filthy sleeping bag. He glares at the aged shoppers passing by, intimidating them into throwing coins into the Styrofoam coffee cup he uses as a begging bowl.

When Giles has collected a few Euros, he buys himself a bottle of cheap red wine at the Franprix. At most hours of the day, there is a long lineup at the cash register, each customer militantly watching for anyone trying to butt in, but nobody gives Giles any trouble when he crashes to the front of the line; he is, quite frankly, too stinky and crazy to cross.

Once outside, Giles returns to his post where he offers sartorial criticisms to passersby. "Hey, those slacks make your ass look big. You call that a hat? I've seen better rat nests."

I am out on a Tuesday morning on my way to the butcher shop when I notice Giles is already into his third bottle of Château Ruby. During one of his frequent blackouts, someone's dog has dropped a pile directly in front of his spot. Adding insult to injury, a pedestrian has then trod in it and spread it along the sidewalk in a series of swoops, like a brown endorsement for a well-known pair of sneakers.

Giles is disgusted by this sudden deluge of filth in his personal domain and begins to holler loudly until a policeman comes over to see what the commotion is all about. The beggar indignantly flings his cup of pennies at the mess. "Look what they did to my sidewalk. I demand you clean it up!"

The policeman patiently takes out his walkie-talkie. "We got a mess down here in front of Giles. Can you send a *motocrotte*?"

According to city statistics, there are 200,000 dogs in Paris, and each day, as is their nature, they lay down sixteen tonnes of *crotte*, all of it on the sidewalk. "What," asked the city bureaucrats, "should we do about it?" The normal, logical approach would be to make the owners clean it up, but, as I have noticed by now, "normal" and "logical" are probably the two most underused adjectives in this country. Instead, in a flare of Gallic technological ingenuity that would have impressed Rube Goldberg, the city crossed a vacuum cleaner with a motorcycle. A crack team of poop cleaners was commissioned to swoop down upon the most egregious examples. The brigade, clad in bright green, soon became known as the *motocrottes*, and invitations to appear in parades came pouring in from around the world. Like a posse of mounted leprechauns, they perform daring feats of synchronized riding, all the while cleaning up after any elephants or horses that may have passed ahead.

Needless to say, the *motocrottes* had very little impact on the relentless onslaught. Every year, over six hundred citizens are hospitalized after slipping and falling. An angry coterie of young mothers, tired of their children getting covered in the mess, organized a protest in which they dumped soiled diapers in the Luxembourg Gardens. Others marched on city hall, hurling bags of the offending matter at the statues that crouch in niches on the façade. It might have all come to naught except for an artist who decided to seek out fresh specimens and chalk a victim outline around them and then stick a little French flag on top. Take that, you Paris bureaucrats.

This, *mon ami*, was war. Patrick Delanoë, the mayor of Paris, dutifully launched a massive campaign against the offending lumps. Under his direction, City Hall began to enforce laws already on the books. Owners who were caught not cleaning up after their pets were dinged 180 Euros, with subsequent fines rising to over 400 Euros.

But Parisian dog owners don't give up that easily. The predictable response for them has been to find a nice small street, like rue Barbette, where they can keep a close eye peeled for *les flics* as their poodles do their business. As a result, our lane has become an obstacle course in which I risk twisted limbs and grotty shoes every time I step out the door. Perhaps I will glue some blue and red ribbons to a dog biscuit and launch my own crusade, awarding the *Crotte d'honneur* to the filthiest streets in Paris.

Paris bans most large-scale billboards from the centre of town, but ever since the days of Toulouse-Lautrec, the city has been a haven for posters. Many of them are quite original and eye-catching, such as the coffee advertisement featuring a woman in a bright pink rubber facemask, a tiny cup of espresso perched on her protruding tongue like a lozenge. Some are confusing, such as the black and white handbill glued to a derelict shop window showing an arrow embedded in the torso of a young man.

The Paris Metro uses a cartoon character called *Petit Lapin*, or Mr. Bunny Rabbit, to illustrate the dangers of the subway system. Normally, he is depicted in posters running on the platform or getting his hand caught in the doors. A local AIDS awareness group, getting into the spirit of things, decide to appropriate *Petit Lapin* when they print up a poster promoting the use of condoms. In it, Mr. Bunny Rabbit blissfully sodomizes a companion. Even though it is unclear whether they are on the Metro or not, the transportation authorities order the posters taken down, and Mr. Bunny Rabbit returns to more traditional forms of dangerous behaviour.

Many of the posters are erotic. As though driving in Paris isn't distracting enough, Paris advertisers feel the need to place soft-core porn right next to the fast lane. A typical ad features a long-legged woman in a skimpy outfit bending over to fondle her leather high heels. Promotions for slimming potions prefer naked models clamping clothes pegs to their svelte derrières. Judging from the state of the steel poles lining the curb in the downstream direction, they both seem to have a similar impression on drivers.

In fact, the surfeit of T&A on public roads can get a bit much. Lately, activists have begun to protest the exploitation of women by defacing posters. I pass a large billboard in the Metro promoting a lingerie sale at a department store in town. The young female model, wearing a skimpy bra and panty set and high heels, is lifting a tray of lasagna from her oven. Someone has slapped a bright yellow triangular sticker with the word *Sexisme!* on her cleavage. I wonder if they are protesting the fact that she is semi-naked or cooking dinner?

Of course, no election campaign would be complete without posters, and the official start of French presidential elections in mid-March is marked by the appearance of grimly smiling visages all over town. President Chirac, amid a scandal over kickbacks while he was mayor of Paris, announces that he will accede to the popular will of the people and once again reluctantly run for office, thus, coincidentally, retaining his immunity from prosecution. Prime Minister Jospin, equally modest, announces that he, too, might be persuaded to defer his long-held desire to start a garlic patch and contest the issue on behalf of all good socialists.

Eagerly, I await the emergence of a campaign platform. Will the voters demand reduced unemployment? An end to strikes in the public sector? A reduction in crime?

Hell, no. Voters want to know who is going to fix their traffic tickets. Ever since 1965, when Charles de Gaulle instigated the gesture, the triumphant candidate has issued a blanket amnesty cancelling outstanding *procès-verbaux*. Which tickets, they want to know, would each candidate forgive?

The issue isn't trivial. Parking is virtually non-existent in Paris. Formerly, there was lots of parking space available on the sidewalks, but the city perversely decided to reserve those areas for pedestrians and put steel kingpins into the curbs every three metres. The few spots still available are crammed with Peugeots and Citroëns to the point where there is less than fifteen centimetres between cars, a distance from which it is virtually impossible to extricate yourself without a stick of dynamite. And when even those spaces are gone, there is no alternative but to park in the white-striped pedestrian crossings. The meter maids, blue bowler hats aggressively cocked to one side, wait in ambush for such escapades, gleefully papering windshields with high denomination fines.

Moving violations are also rife. The Marais is festooned with one-way streets in a vain attempt to reduce the traffic congestion on its tiny lanes. Parisian drivers have their own way of interpreting the law, however, and a one-way street only means that a car should be pointing in the right direction, not necessarily moving in the right direction. They see nothing wrong with reversing at high speed using only the rear-view mirror to steer their way. Curiously, the traffic police don't quite agree with this interpretation and are more than happy to issue a summons to miscreants. A presidential term, which is now five years, gives the average French driver the opportunity to accumulate several thousand Euros worth of fines.

Not everyone, of course, is in favour of the amnesty. Most drivers dutifully pay their fines and resent those scofflaws who run up horrific tabs. More to the point, road safety groups fulminate against the practice, stating quite rightly that the French do not need any more incentives to drive badly. As a result, the candidates dance around the issue like a pretty whore on Sunday, but everyone knows that all of those voters eagerly awaiting the presidential hocus-pocus that will magically make their tickets disappear will eventually make both candidates succumb.

There is a driving school in the Marais called, oxymoronically, *Le Fun Drive*. I can imagine that learning to drive a car in Paris is about as much fun as learning to milk viper venom in Bangkok. Are the instructors truly happy, or are they so loaded on Prozac that they can laugh in the face of death?

More than likely, it's just the typical Parisian response to authority. The French Academy, or Académie Française, was founded by the anal Cardinal Richelieu in 1635. In addition to awarding literary prizes, its forty "immortals" edit the official French dictionary and then, in officious bulletins, tell everybody exactly how the language should be used. A computer, for instance, is designated as an *ordinateur*.

For their part, the French people nod gravely at such pronouncements and then do exactly as they please. The end of the week is not referred to as the official *fin de semaine*, but *le weekend*, often shortened in salutations to *bon wee*.

To the Académie Française's undoubted chagrin, English is used wherever and whenever it catches the common whim. There has been a fad lately for young Parisian women to buy T-shirts from Taiwan emblazoned with English sayings, something the residents of this Asian island have been pursuing with glee for many years. I once visited Taipei, and my favourite T-shirt said "Kiss me, Fire Hydrant." Since then, the Taiwanese have graduated to more salacious sayings. As I walk past Notre-Dame cathedral, I see a woman wearing a sleeveless pink tank-top with "Queen Bitch" spelled out in sequins. What's next? "Bring Back the 10-Franc Blowjob?"

Parisians have three questions they always ask foreigners. "Where are you from?" "How long have you been in France?" And, most important, "What do you think of Paris?" Parisians are among the most worldly and sophisticated people I have ever met, but they never, ever miss a chance to ask visitors, in a mixture of vanity and childish anticipation, what they think of their great city. It's charmingly endearing, in an egotistical way.

I always surprise them on the third question. "I love Paris."

This is invariably met with undisguised disbelief. "You *do*? Why?"

"Because the people are so friendly."

At this point they think I am pulling their baguette, but it's the truth. Parisians like to be thought of as brusque and cynical and rude, but they don't hold a *bougie* to Londoners. Now, there's a tough crew. A true Londoner will back over you with his car and then get road rage when you bleed on his tires.

Coincidentally, it is a damp, foggy, Thames-like evening, and the weather has put us in the mood for some cheering up. After a quick glass of champagne, we head out in search of somewhere to eat. There is little enthusiasm for ranging too far afield looking for the perfect little bistro in filthy weather such as this. Tonight we decide that proximity rates far above any stars Michelin might deem prudent to award.

In many cities, this sort of behaviour might be an invitation to botulism. In London, searching for something to eat is a nasty choice between expensive and arrogant, or cheap and dangerous; breaded veal is the intestinal version of Russian roulette. In contrast, exploring for a new place to eat in Paris is a joy; shall it be mouth-watering lamb roasted in rosemary, or perhaps duck in orange liqueur sauce? Who cares? Just walk into the nearest brasserie and order the special of the day and a bottle of the house red, and prepare to be amazed.

We no sooner round the corner onto rue Vieille du Temple than we spot Restaurant Robert & Louise amid the swirling mist. I had passed along this stretch of road countless times but had never made much note of its presence. A tiny signboard decorated with leaping flames of fire juts out from a thicket of ivy over the doorway. The windows, covered with red and white checked curtains, obscure the business within. The menu in the window is short on details. A notice forewarns "no credit cards are accepted." The only indication that the restaurant is open for business is the tiny square of white cardboard, labelled *fermé*, that has been turned to its blank side. I can hardly imagine a more cavalier attitude to self-promotion in all of Paris. We immediately decide to give it a try.

We are met at the door by the head waitress who shakes her head gravely when we reveal we have no dinner reservations. She escorts us to a table for two, a tiny, semi-circular affair designed for circus performers. We squeeze past the adjacent patrons and make ourselves as comfortable as possible in the spartan cane chairs.

I look around the room and conclude that only the French can make decrepitude so charming. The oak beams holding up the roof are in such terrible condition that even the woodworms have decamped. The furniture appears to have been hewn from logs by unemployed catapult builders.

The proprietors are similarly antique. Robert, with a shock of white hair and stooped shoulders, holds court at a dining table at the back of the restaurant near a roaring fireplace. A large, raw rib roast rests upon the table along with a cutting board and knife. When a patron orders an entrecôte, Robert cuts the requisite amount and then hands it to the chef, who salts and peppers the meat before placing it in the *cheminée*, a flat, iron griddle in the fireplace.

Louise shuffles around the restaurant in her house slippers placing wooden plates and razor sharp cutlery on the tables. When she comes to take our order, she explains that they have run the restaurant for the last forty years in the manner of the original establishment, built shortly after 1650. The only significant changes over the interceding centuries appeared to be the addition of a large fridge and the table fork.

We choose the tantalizingly labelled entrecôte for two. I also request an assortment of escargots and veal head, but Louise ignores my entreaties for appetizers. "The entrecôte will be sufficient," she explains, and promptly commands Robert to open a Brouilly for our table.

Gladly abandoning his butchery duties, Robert advances

to the bar at the front of the restaurant and pours himself a restorative glass of red wine before engaging in the laborious task of opening the Brouilly. He relishes his duties, carefully removing the lead wrapper and then examining the top of the cork for signs of ignoble mould, before extracting the cork with a spindly screw.

The entrecôte arrives shortly thereafter, accompanied by a salad, a large plate of pan-fried potatoes, and a small black poodle named Isaiah, who positions himself strategically below the roast beef. Unfortunately for Isaiah, the meat has been seared to perfection on the outside while retaining a pink, tender juiciness on the inside, and we selfishly reduce the roast to its component rib.

After the main course, Louise returns to ask us if we would like a cheese plate or a dessert plate.

"What is in the cheese plate?" I ask.

Louise ponders for a moment. "Cheese."

"And the dessert plate?"

"Why, dessert, of course."

With this clarification, we order the cheese plate which, as promised, contains cheese, in this case slices of Brie, Camembert, and a delicious mouldy something in the fashion of Gorgonzola. By the end of the meal, we are too full to even find room for coffee. Amid hearty praise for the food, we pay the bill and make our way back out into the swirling mists, glad for the umpteenth time that we are living in the greatest culinary city in the world.

This spring, *Pâques*, or Easter Sunday, falls on the last day of March. Saint-Paul–Saint-Louis church, its magnificent, grimy façade gussied up with a large lavender banner, is filled to capacity with the citizens of the Marais, each one making up for the fifteen Sundays since Christmas when they have had to attend engagements more pressing than Mass.

I am told it wasn't always so. When the original parish church was finished in 1641, the Jesuit Bourdaloue, who could preach for three hours non-stop, was an instant hit. His sermons were so popular that women would send their servants at 5 AM to reserve a seat for the afternoon show. They brought along little potties to tuck under the pew so that their bladders didn't burst. To this day, a bedpan in the Marais is still called a *Bourdaloue*.

Right next door to the church is a tiny greengrocer's shop, run by Monsieur Beouf and his beet-faced wife. Easter also marks the annual re-emergence of another heavenly gift, the first new potatoes. Monsieur Beouf points to a box in which sits a hatful of tiny spheres, each about the size of a ping-pong ball. "These are the new *Sirtimas*." He kisses the tips of his fingers. "They are the best. And at only 12 Euros a kilo, a real steal."

That's the problem with food retailers in this town—they put the average heroin pusher to shame. "How much harm can it be to try it just once, monsieur?" I gaze down at his focus of adoration, a collection of brownish green spheres with spots of skin peeling off. Not the most appetizing spuds I have ever seen, I think, but, at what I calculate to be around 1 Euro per pound, undeniably the most expensive. Against my better judgment, I buy a kilo.

When I get home, I do a little internet research on my new potatoes. It turns out they are grown on the tiny island of Noirmoutier, sitting some ten kilometres off the west coast of France. This wind-swept chunk of rock and kelp was bereft of all life except monks until the arrival of tubers from the New

World. Apparently, the moderating influence of the Atlantic combined with the sandy coastal soils creates ideal conditions for spring potatoes, and each year, at Candlemas, farmers plant their crop on the five hundred or so hectares of choice land. Three months later, they begin to dig up the first tiny spuds and speed them along to the waiting gourmets of Europe. "Exceptional it is," notes the Noirmoutier website, "by its fairness, its juicy flesh, and its fruity taste." I am ready to lick the picture on my screen right then and there.

I decide that salmon would be a perfect accompaniment to my starchy nuggets of gold. I dutifully wander up to rue de Bretagne, where our *poissonnier*, an intense, stork-like man, is busy laying out a display of extremely ugly fish with a set of teeth that would do a *Tyrannosaurus rex* proud. His salmon is so fresh that it positively glows, and he carefully cleans the skin and bones from two thick, juicy filets.

Normally, I grill salmon on the barbecue, but since barbecuing and pheasant hunting are two activities I normally avoid indoors, I defer to the grill pan. After marinating the filets in a mixture of molasses sugar, soy sauce, mustard, and fresh ground pepper, I lightly brown them in the grill pan. At the same time, I boil the Noirmoutiers and flavour them with butter and fresh parsley.

As promised by Monsieur Boeuf, the new potatoes are the best I have ever tasted. Each orb combines the essence of buttery cream with the freshness of warm springtime zephyrs. As we consume every last Noirmoutier, I am filled with an intense, irresistible desire for more. How much, I wonder, would the city pawnshop give me for the Maestro's TV?

AVRIL

The French traditionally celebrate April Fools Day by secretly trying to stick a paper fish on their victim's back. This is not nearly as funny as, say, putting clear plastic wrap over the top of a toilet bowl, but sometimes the French manage to come up with something better without even trying. According to *Le Parisien*, French customs agents decided this year to celebrate 1 April by going on a *manifestation*, or work-to-rule. The plan was to check every single bag of every single passenger getting on the Eurostar train to London, a process that would delay departures by several hours and, presumably, generate endless mirth. It turns out the big trick was on a Senegalese diplomat who didn't know the difference between a *manifestation* and a *grève*, or work stoppage, and decided it was a good day to smuggle thirty kilograms of cocaine into the United Kingdom. Since he was accredited to Gabon and not France, the customs agents had no alternative than to throw him in jail. Not surprisingly, his error was greeted with no small amount of hilarity by the local citizenry.

Actually, the average Parisian is a lot less cynical than you might think, but it also helps if his conscience is pricked now and again. Paris, it seems, is in contention with Beijing to host the 2008 Summer Olympics. Just before the site is to be announced, however, the government of China issues a travel advisory to its citizens warning them not to travel to Paris, because it isn't safe.

The advisory stings the French for two reasons. First, it is issued by a regime that exercises even more state control than its own, and second, it is true. Thieves, and pickpockets especially, have been targeting Asian visitors, dashing off with their purses and ruining their holidays. The police are ordered by the president to crack down on cut-purses. Several hundred *flics* are promptly dispatched to infiltrate the underworld.

They could have saved a lot of effort by simply hanging out in the Châtelet. With six different lines intersecting in a vast spaghetti of interconnecting tunnels, the Metro station is a veritable rat's nest of thieves. Linda and I are travelling through the Châtelet a few days later when we spot a group of suspicious-looking youngsters. The kids, some no more than eleven years of age, make their way to our platform. The train driver, aware of their presence, makes an announcement that there are pickpockets in the area, but the warning is so ubiquitous that regular passengers no longer even hear it.

We lose sight of the thieves, but move well away from the doorways anyway. The doors are about to close when the leader of the pack, a boy of around sixteen, squeezes his way onto the train and grabs an Asian woman's shoulder bag. She lets out a shriek as he flees. Or, at least, as he tries to flee. A young Frenchman runs after the thief, catching him before he gets too far. He holds the boy in a headlock while his girlfriend alerts the train driver to call the police. The lad attempts to throw the purse onto the tracks under the train, but another passenger takes it from him and gives it back to the victim. Everyone in the car turns to one another with big, satisfied grins. Put some soy sauce on your travel advisory warning *et mangez-le, camarade.*

Considering the general state of alert involving mad bombers, juvenile pickpockets, and other nefarious riff-raff, it is with some surprise that I note a woman lugging a large bag of swords along rue Vieille du Temple the following afternoon. I follow her to the Blancs Manteaux gymnasium, where several dozen men and women in white fencing uniforms and wire mesh masks are hopping about energetically in armed combat.

Against all better judgment, I enter. Near the doorway stands a booth filled with sparring paraphernalia. In addition to how-to books and pointy swords, there is a charming display of French postcards, taken at the turn of the century, featuring two largely naked women demonstrating various duelling poses. A small man with a very large handlebar mustache is standing at the booth. A nametag on his lapel identifies him as Jacques, the *maître d'armes*, or fencing instructor.

We strike up a conversation. According to Jacques, the rapier, invented in 1606 by an Italian, quickly became much more popular than the traditional sword. To explain why, he steps out from behind the booth to wave an invisible cutlass in my general direction. "Imagine you are a man-of-arms with a heavy broadsword." I furrow my brow and comply. "While you lift it up to strike, your opponent penetrates you with the rapier." He rolls his eyes up and grimaces in mortal pain. "You are soon dead—that is very bad, no?"

I agree that is very bad, yes, and Jacques goes on to explain how the rapier was turned into the shorter épée by, as is so often the case, French fashion designers. In the second half of the seventeenth century, the court of Louis XIV set the fashion of silk stockings, breeches, and brocaded coats. A long, trailing rapier was simply unsuitable, and the forebears of John Galliano decreed the wearing of a short, light weapon.

Unfortunately, the shorter, more refined sword elicited

unwarranted comparisons with the wearer's personal equipment, and duels soon proliferated. Jacques shakes his mustache in weary recollection. "The place des Vosges, that was a very special place for duels. Every king and cardinal from Louis XIII tried to stop the practice, but the edicts were universally ignored, and a tremendous carnage ensued. They say that ten thousand men died in ten years in Paris."

I express, as politely as possible, my incredulity at the statistic.

Jacques's eyes fly wide open at the affront. "It is true! You see, every duelist was accompanied by two seconds. An argument over procedure would ensue, and soon you had all six men fighting." Jacques flings his right arm hither and yon, doing his best to mimic a melee. "Before they could be broken up, four men might be dead."

A cursory investigation of contemporary accounts shows that Jacques's version of events was long on romance but a tad short of the mark. The épée probably originated in Italy, and Louis XIV was more noted for his severe sanctions against duelling than its promotion. The place des Vosges was indeed notorious for its duels, but estimates during the heyday of swordplay in the early seventeenth century place deaths at something like a dozen a month for all of France, well short of Jacques's estimate.

Still Jacques's stories did pique my interest in the place des Vosges, located a few blocks east of rue Barbette. Completed in 1612, it was the original luxury condo project, with thirty-six aristocratic pavilions done in white stone and red brick around a large, open square. Today, it has been completely restored and is lined with art galleries, restaurants, and *brocanteur* shops. On hot sunny days, the students who live in the district congregate near the fountains in the square to see and to be seen. When I arrive, a young Japanese woman is spread out on the grass, her blue jeans pulled down low to show off a pair of plaid bloomers. One of the legs on her pants has also been cut off, the better to display a bright red stocking. Her hair is braided into half a dozen tiny pigtails randomly distributed over her head. I surmise that the fashion police are on *grève* today.

In the centre of the square, Janice is explaining the sad tale of Henri II and the errant jousting lance to a dozen Bavarian dentists. She finishes her story and asks if they have any questions. One of the tourists, wearing a fake orange tan that nicely complements his Birkenstock sandals and white socks, puts up his hand. "It hurt, jah?"

"No, not much." Janice blinks slowly, as if to savour the vision of a dentist getting a large lance stuck in a moist, sensitive spot. After the lecture, I ask her about where the rapier duels were held.

"Over there, in front of #21, where Cardinal Richelieu lived."

"Wasn't he against duels?"

"Very much. That's why they held them under his nose."

The most famous resident of the place des Vosges, who never died in a duel or got stuck in the eye, was Victor Hugo. The author of the *Hunchback of Notre Dame* lived in number 9, from 1832 to 1848. I thank Janice and walk over to the home, which is open as a museum and has been restored with many of Hugo's original furnishings and decorations.

The main entrance, a set of thick double oak doors, leads through a foyer to the back courtyard, now a school playground. To the left, a long set of wood and wrought-iron stairs wends upwards in stately fashion to the drawing room and bedrooms. The layout of the mansion follows the style typical of the seventeenth century. There is no hallway, just a series of grand rooms connected by double doors.

He may have been a laureate of literature, but it turns out that Victor had a somewhat plebian taste for bright red silk wallpaper and gaudy velvet curtains. He also had a fondness for medieval furniture, and *brocanteurs* were always showing up at his doorway with the latest find, often, I suspect, unbolted from a rural church the evening before. In his bedroom stands a tiny four-poster in the style of Louis XIII, in which he died in 1885. Over a million people came to see him lying in state at Notre-Dame before he was carried to his final resting place in the Panthéon.

I am standing on pont de l'Archevêché, the starting point of Hugo's procession and Monique's current studio, thinking about nothing in particular. It is a cloudy, joyless Monday afternoon, but the dull weather hasn't discouraged a dozen immense buses from disgorging tourists and diesel fumes in equally pleasing amounts on the east side of the cathedral.

Monique looks up from her canvas. "Have you seen them?"

I look around, unsure. Does she mean the tour group of fat women in matching pink sweaters with a logo that looks like someone getting in-vitro fertilization? "Who?"

"The falcons." She points up toward a tiny speck circling above the twin towers of Notre-Dame. "There's a nest in the belfry." Nothing less than the Ornithological Centre for the Ile de France has set up a closed-circuit TV camera to observe the nest. At Monique's suggestion, I push through the crowds in place Jean XXIII and make my way toward their white tent.

Inside the tent, a TV screen shows the chicks as they sit in their twiggy home awaiting the return of their mother. A biologist explains that the falcons have already chased all the pigeons away from the square in search of food. I think this is an excellent idea and suggest, perhaps, that the centre might want to install a den of lions to chase off all the tourists as well. The biologist gives me a look that suggests a hasty departure from his tent is in order.

Actually, the tradition of tossing unwanted visitors to carnivores goes back a long way in Paris. In the nineteenth century, archeologists excavating a Roman amphitheatre near the Pantheon concluded from fossilized fecal deposits that it was used for feeding errant Gauls to the lions almost two millennia ago. In addition, some local parishioners say the church of Saint-Gervais–Saint-Protais, located in a leafy square just east of the Hôtel de Ville, is dedicated to two Christian brothers who met a similar end by Nero's hand. The story is unlikely. When Saint-Ambroise dug up their remains near Milan in the fourth century, the bodies were found to be very well preserved, except for the effects of scourging and decapitation. No evidence of gnawing was observed.

The church itself is an oasis of calm in the sea of noise that surrounds it—at least most of the time. A stained glass window in a south-facing alcove commemorates a tragedy that took place on Good Friday, 1918. The Germans, dug-in 160 kilometres east of Paris, fired a Big Bertha cannon at the town. Six minutes later, a shell crashed into the roof, killing one hundred parishioners as they knelt at the carved pews.

None of this distracted me from my appointed task, a visit to rue François Miron. The street, named after Henry IV's chief of the army, is famous for two things: Israel's Epicerie and the Hôtel de Beauvais. When I arrive at the Hôtel de Beauvais, the façade is covered in scaffolding, and the building is closed to visitors. I am disappointed, as the building clearly has one of the most interesting pedigrees in the Marais. The hôtel was built in 1657 by Lady Catherine Bellier. Known as One-eyed Kate, she was the hunch-backed lady-in-waiting of Anne of Austria. While not the greatest woman to look at, even with one eye closed and the other squinting, she had an abundance of love for the young and was the first woman to demonstrate the amorous facts of life to a sixteen-year-old Louis XIV. Louis didn't forget such favours, and when he became king a few years later, it is said he honoured her with the funds to build the hôtel.

Fortunately, Israel's isn't under renovation or closed for a Jewish holiday. I march through the front door, past the baskets of dried apricots, basmati rice, and couscous. It is literally crammed to the rafters with every herb, spice, and sauce imaginable, and is virtually the only place in town with a reliable source of *pappadums*, a lentil-based bread, as well as *garam masala*, a mix of ground cinnamon, cloves, and curry powder. The old man who operates the store has a serious charm deficit when it comes to backpackers trying to squeeze past immense stacks of kitchen ceramics, but he doesn't seem to mind if food nerds waste endless hours fondling the pickles and reading the ingredients on Thai fish sauce bottles. Thai fish sauce is made from fermented anchovies, in case you're interested.

I arrive home burdened down with spices from the Far East only to learn that we are going out for dinner that evening. Jim has a friend in town for a visit and wants to meet up with Linda and me for cocktails and dinner. According to Vogue magazine, Madonna likes to hang out at the Buddha Bar when she is in town. Since celebrities appreciate the opportunity to mingle with normal folk, we decide to oblige her and head down to place de la Concorde.

Linda and I arrive early and decide to scout about. The main room, with a nine-metre ceiling, is completely encircled by a balcony. The walls are painted a deep burgundy, and the lighting shines almost exclusively from candles placed on the tables. We quickly discover that this makes reading the cocktail menu almost as easy as spotting Madonna. I am regretting leaving my flashlight at home when the waitress eventually spots us through the gloom. I order the house martini, a mix of vodka, Grand Marnier, and fresh ginger, and Linda requests a Bellini, a blend of champagne and peach nectar.

No doubt James Bond would have gagged at the effrontery, but I pronounce my ginger cocktail fine, except perhaps for the need of a little more fish sauce. Linda, on the other hand, takes one sip and calls the waitress back. "This isn't a Bellini."

The waitress shakes her head in utter disbelief. "No?"

"No. A Bellini has peach nectar in it. This drink has cranberries."

The waitress obligingly takes it back to the bar, dumps out half the drink and pours in more cranberry juice. This might have worked quite well with a turkey canapé, but the Buddha Bar has unwisely opted for shrimp crackers, and the two do not blend well on the palate.

Fortunately, Jim arrives with his friend Gwen. The latter takes one look at our cocktails and immediately orders a bottle of Veuve Clicquot champagne. Gwen, it turns out, is an international lawyer recently arrived from Houston. A Malaysian by birth, she combines a vibrant, take-charge personality with an uncanny lack of driving skill. As we sip our drinks, Jim tells me she once took two doors off a Jaguar with the bumper of her car. I must ask someday if it was her front or rear bumper.

We are escorted downstairs to the main hall, which is large enough to seat two hundred diners, including a 4.5-metre statue of Buddha. It isn't the skeletal Buddha, which would have been a little off-putting for the clientele, nor is it the happy, chubby Buddha, which would have been inappropriate for the California-fusion-inspired, low fat menu. It is a politically correct, buff Buddha with a six-pack for pecs.

The restaurant, if anything, is even gloomier than the bar, which I conclude is either a nod to ambience or a subtle ploy to conceal the prices. Our waiter, who is wearing a black T-shirt emblazoned with "Buddha Bar" in large red script, lest we forget where we are, thinks Gwen's suggestion to bring everyone's main dish at the same time quite novel, and goes off to share this tidbit with his peers. The main course, when it eventually appears, proves to be somewhat larger and more enjoyable than the starters, but by this time the manager has his eye on the second sitting and the plates are snatched up from our laps as soon as we are done. The total tab, which arrives almost immediately, is sufficient to cremate a monastery. On the way out, I think I spot Madonna in the gift shop purchasing an authentic Buddha Bar ashtray, but it is too gloomy to be sure.

I step out my front door the following morning and survey the street. The wonderful thing about the Marais is that you can point your feet in any direction of the compass, content with the knowledge that some adventure awaits in that direction. But where should I go today? To the north, where a stable of exotic animals awaits behind the Winter Circus? What about to the west, where an exhibit of French painter Jean Dubuffet's art is being shown in the Georges Pompidou Centre? Or maybe to the south, to rummage through the stacks of pornographic ceramic figurines at the five-and-dime store on rue de Rivoli? A warm breeze blowing the scent of plum blossoms along rue Barbette solves my predicament. I follow my nose in an easterly direction.

As I round the corner onto rue Elzévir, I pass a crew of workmen standing in front of the neighbourhood *horodateur*. The city parking meters, situated one to a block, are steel rectangular boxes mounted on sturdy posts. Residents pay fifty cents a day to park, while visitors must shell out 2 Euros per hour. A technician is busy fitting a metal plate over a jagged hole that has been cut, with great effort, into the corner of the machine. Who, I wonder aloud, would go to all that trouble?

The supervisor, a white-haired man in his fifties, pulls the cigarette out of his mouth. "Thieves." He consults his clipboard. "They hit over fifty machines last night."

"How much is in each machine?"

The supervisor shrugs. "Maybe 5 Euros."

No wonder they prefer picking pockets. When I reach rue Pavée in the Jewish section of the Marais, I lose the trail of the plum blossom scent. Standing on the sidewalk, I observe two heavyset men in long, curly beards and black fedoras discussing either nuances of the Torah, or perhaps the best place to get a blintz. A trio of aged women in cheap cotton scarves sit in front of the synagogue begging coins and comparing teeth. A very tall man from Senegal, a *Sephardim*, wheels a dolly filled with bags of potato chips down the centre of the street.

The one thing I can't see is the blossoming plum tree. I am suddenly struck by the difference between streetscapes in Paris and North America—in Paris there isn't a slice of green anywhere in sight. Growing up in Canada, I am used to wide swaths of lawn, large ambling parks, and immense trees. Here, there's not so much as a blade of grass to be seen. Buildings don't just abut right against the street, they hang over the gutter like a seasick drunk, barring any glimmer of sunshine that might errantly succour a weed growing from the many cracks in the pavement.

That's not to say there is no public greenery *anywhere* in the Marais. The Templars Square, in front of the 3rd arrondissement's city hall, was the site of the monastic order's main *donjon* until the king of France roasted the lot of them on a spit for practicing sorcery without a licence. If it's any consolation to the Templars, the square is now filled with duck ponds, yellow forsythia bushes, and beds of tulips.

My favourite public garden is attached to the Hôtel de Sens, located near the Pont Marie Metro station just north of the Seine. The yard features intricately patterned boxwood hedges interspersed with beds of brilliant yellow tulips in spring. The medieval mansion itself, now fully restored, was built in the late fifteenth century and served as a home for Queen Margot, the wife of Henry IV and a great lover of food. In those days, wide ruffs were the fashion, and local gossip says she had special, long-handled spoons made to reach her mouth. The spoons worked so well that all the doors had to be widened to accommodate her bulk. During the French Revolution, the building was made into a jam factory, and after the Second World War, before the garden was restored, local citizens grew cabbage on the grounds.

In the absence of green space, residents of the Marais who wish to mollify their green thumbs have an alternative outlet: the window box. As I turn onto rue Barbette, I catch sight of the bright red geraniums, purple petunias, and yellow chrysanthemums cascading down the sides of ancient apartments. Inspired, I examine the windows in our living room. Right at the base, guarded by a wrought-iron railing, is a tiny space about 120 centimetres wide and 30 centimetres deep—perfect for a garden. I grab my caddy and hurry down to BHV.

The basement of the department store is a home repair heaven with every conceivable tool and piece of hardware in stock. I had been told by Madame Greco that a garden centre, complete with sacks of soil, spades, and planters, is tucked into one corner, but it is nowhere in sight. This is not necessarily discouraging; following the basic tenets of French retail theory, the entire floor is a jam of cordless handsaws, steel security blinds, and drill bits. I tie a piece of twine to the base of the escalator and set off in search of mulch.

One good thing about garden centres is they smell the same the world over. After two or three dead ends, I finally detect the unmistakable odour of cedar boards and slug bait. There, stacked before me, is a vast array of decorative urns, all finely wrought in highest-quality PVC. I purchase four boxes, two for the front windows and two for the kitchen windows, along with a large bag of soil. There is a picture of a contented cow, not unlike those at the butcher's, smiling into the camera as it energetically produces soil-to-be.

Now, what to plant? I head down to the Marché aux Fleurs et aux Oiseaux on Ile de la Cité where, tucked between the main police station and the courts of justice, vendors sell a wide assortment of flora and fauna. For the front window boxes, which will get abundant sunshine, I purchase red geraniums, blue lobelia, and white petunias. I settle upon rosemary, chives, oregano, thyme, and basil for the kitchen.

Placing the boxes directly on the window ledges, I begin to potter about. As I pull the petunias out, a clump of dirt rolls off the ledge and drops directly into the cleavage of a woman passing by on the street below. Now, I ask you, what are the odds? Even if I had tried fifty times to do it on purpose, I bet I would never have succeeded, even once. I try to explain this to the woman, but she shouts some of the things that Madame Laglace used to say in my Grade 7 French class. Ah, the benefits of an education.

I finish just as Madame Greco is coming back from the Bastille market with her oranges and cabbage. "Ah, that looks good—very patriotic! Just in time for the elections!" Without realizing it, I had picked the colours of the French flag.

Every five years, the nation goes to the polls to choose a new president. Anyone who can get 500 of the country's 35,000 mayors to sign their nomination form is eligible to run in the first round, but only the top two finishers can enter the second round. The process is not dissimilar to an international soccer tournament, complete with tear gas.

The first round falls upon the last Sunday in April. Even though there are sixteen candidates spanning the political spectrum, from left-wing Trotskyites to right-wing Loonies, the presidential election is supposed to be a sleepwalk, with only two mainstream candidates, Prime Minister Lionel Jospin, a socialist, and President Jacques Chirac, a moderate conservative, seriously challenging for the post. By common agreement, they avoid any debate over the issues that matter, including rising crime, immigrant unemployment, anti-Semitism, and their own pending jail terms.

The only colour in the race comes from the defacement of the campaign posters stuck to metal plaques outside the voting offices. Chirac, plagued by scandals from his days as mayor of Paris, has *super-menteur*—super liar—scribbled on his fore-head. Jean-Marie Le Pen, a neo-Fascist, has the predictable black handlebar mustache added to his upper lip. Only Jospin, a bland, colourless technocrat, seems to be ignored by the graffiti artists.

Voting day for round one is warm and sunny in Paris, and I walk over to the Bastille in search of a *brocante* that is being held in the wide, shaded park that runs down the centre of boulevard Richard Lenoir. The Bastille on Sunday is normally a big, festive traffic circle with hundreds of diners lounging away the hours at the sidewalk restaurants, but not today. A large crowd of students gathers in unorganized knots, occasionally taking up the chant "Down with Le Pen." The ornate column commemorating the uprising of July 1830 has been defaced by graffiti. Pieces of Plexiglass cling jaggedly to the frame of a bus stop. A young man in a red shirt climbs onto the roof of a van and sprays "Fuck the Fascists" on the side of a building. When several men pull up steel kingpins from the side of the road and begin bashing parked cars, a phalanx of riot police advance. The crowd throws bottles and stones, and the police respond with tear gas. I am beginning to get the general impression that something unusual may have happened.

I hurry back home and turn on the TV. Jospin has been pipped at the polls by Le Pen. The stations are jammed with talking heads bemoaning the international black eye this has caused France. Only Le Pen supporters seem jubilant, confirmed by shots of men with shaved heads cheering in the streets.

What, I wonder, had gone so badly wrong? Bernard had been a big help explaining the French electoral system to me before, so I hurry down the next morning to see what he has to say about this latest development.

The *caviste* is standing in front of his store, his head hung low. "A lot of people didn't vote, including me—I am ashamed," he admits.

"Is this what French people really think?"

"No. It's not the right image of France. The voters did wrong." Bernard sighs. "Now they are going to have to work very hard to make it right."

MAI

The first of May is celebrated with *muguets*, or lily of the valley. Over sixty million sprigs of tiny white flowers are grown annually in Brittany, then sold on every street corner by itinerant vendors at 3 Euros a bunch. They smell like a funeral parlor, but that doesn't deter virtually anyone in France from buying them to give to friends and family. Perhaps they're trying to tell each other something? I ask the young vendor standing on the corner of rue Vieille du Temple and rue des Francs-Bourgeois for an explanation, and he says that it is a sign of affection, but then he has the same ginger hair shade as Natalie the wine merchant does, so I wonder. I buy some for Linda anyway.

It is a beautiful day and we decide to dine outside in place du Marché Sainte-Catherine, where a handful of plane trees provide shade for the French bistro, Jewish deli, and Korean restaurant that cluster around the perimeter like a culinary UN. We had been to the bistro before, and although the food was good, the waiters were far too much in love with their own reflections to waste time fussing with customers. We don't feel like eating a bagel so, in honour of Seoul's upcoming hosting of the soccer World Cup, we sit down at the Korean restaurant and order a steamboat, the house specialty.

A steamboat is a curved steel bowl that resembles the

hubcap of an old Ford coupe: high in the centre with a deep well around the rim. It is very popular down Asia way because there is no possibility of culinary hanky-panky going on behind your back. The waiter brings the whole show right out to your table. Beef strips are laid across the top, along with cabbage, sliced tomatoes, and zucchini, and a sweet beef broth is poured into the rim. The steamboat is then placed upon a portable gas burner that cooks the meal right at your table.

We are industriously picking away at the various succulent portions, relishing the taste of the repast and gustatory peace and quiet of the square, when our reveries are interrupted by raucous students marching down nearby rue de Rivoli. In addition to being Florist Payday, May Day is also the workers' holiday in France and is traditionally celebrated with a parade from place de la République to the Bastille. The participants' causes range from immigrant workers to protecting the rain forest, and the festivity usually features bands, balloon floats, and vendors selling barbecued sausage. For the most part, it is a noisy, jolly affair, with about 20,000 marchers. We decide to join in.

Finishing our meal, we head north toward place de la République. As we get closer to the vast square, however, we encounter a long line of armoured vehicles. Policemen, dressed in Darth Vader carbon-graphite body armour and transparent acrylic shields, stand around checking their flashguns and tear gas launchers. The jolly mood must be infectious.

By the time we reach place de la République, the square is already jammed beyond capacity and the police are turning participants and supporters aside. We march along an adjacent road with a throng of militant pastry chefs until we find a narrow side street that isn't blocked by security forces, and make it out to the main parade.

We are greeted by the shouts of 400,000 marchers. Young and old, black, brown, and white, the entire street is filled with people—four kilometres of protesters, all united in their hatred for the fascist Le Pen. We wiggle our way through the throngs standing on the sidewalk and join the Feminists Against the Extreme Right. Every few minutes, a huge roar starts at one end of the procession and flows down the street, a wave of noise, a cry against oppression. People wave banners with various slogans—"You don't talk Cuisine with Cannibals," and "Crook or Fascist, the choice is yours." We march to the Bastille, where the crowd surges around the July Column. It is very thrilling to experience the passion and commitment of all these people, and we are moved to tears.

When we get back to our apartment on rue Barbette, we bump into Chantal, the Maestro's wife. She is tall and thin as a ballerina, with long black hair. I tell her about our experience with the parade. "We couldn't believe it—one moment we're standing on the sidewalk, and the next, we're right in the middle of the parade, shouting, and singing, and waving along with everyone else."

Chantal's laugh is graceful. "Ah! So you have had a *comble du bonheur*."

I suddenly recall the mysterious name of Jean-Pierre's racehorse. "A what?"

"How would you say in English?" Chantal thinks for a second. "You had a Paris moment."

For the next several days, the streets of the capital are filled with armoured vans rushing to-and-fro, their blue lights angrily flashing as they carry riot police from one hot spot to the next. It is very unnerving and, even more so than with the aftermath of 11 September, the strain begins to show in unlikely places. I stop at Franprix adjacent to the Saint-Paul Metro station to pick up some milk for the morning coffee. One of the refrigerated units has emptied its mechanical bladder onto the linoleum floor, and customers must pick their way down the aisles between a hodge-podge of melting ice cream, copper tubes, and wet cardboard boxes. I detour down the liquor aisle where a clerk is busy picking up shards from a broken bottle of Madeira wine. Standing in the sticky brown ooze, he curses the clumsiness of certain individual shoppers and the general perfidious state of his life. Just then, a bulky woman in a brown cardigan, trying to negotiate her way past the clerk, brushes two more bottles of Burgundy off the adjacent shelf. The clerk places his hands protectively over his genitals as glass shards sail through the air and hollers in frustration. "Look what you're doing!"

"It was an accident!"

"I don't care. You're going to pay, anyway."

"Fascist!"

"Fat Cow!"

The clerk follows her to the cash register where a furious argument ensues. Finally, the woman tosses down her grocery basket and hurls some tasty epithets regarding the clerk's sexual orientation as she storms out of the store. Excitable, these French.

No sooner do I reach home than the sound of emergency sirens fills rue Barbette. I glance outside to see three red pumper trucks from the fire department race up the street and come to a screeching halt in front of the Musée Cognacq-Jay. A dozen men clad in black waterproof coats and gleaming chrome helmets leap from the trucks.

The Cognacq-Jay holds the distinction of being the least

impressive museum in Paris. Located in a modest sixteenth-century mansion, it contains the collection of Ernest Cognacq and his wife, Louise Jay, founders of the Samaritaine department store. Cognacq was an avid collector of ceramic tableaux and oils of cherubic nudes. Although connoisseurs praise his taste, I can't help but note that many of the displayed items look suspiciously like the leftovers still to be found in the store's bargain-basement sales. Regardless, the *pompiers* exercise their duty to protect tacky bric-a-brac. Dragging an impressive array of hoses and axes, and a large plastic tub for disposing of anthrax, they enter through the wide double doors and into the courtyard.

They are met by the director of the museum, a rather thin and serious man sporting a bad toupée. He takes one look at their equipment and his mouth starts to open and close, like a carp's when it is caught on the wrong side of the bowl. The firemen stride past and fan out in search of the nefarious source of the alarm. Fortunately for all concerned, the trouble is a gaggle of teenage visitors cadging a smoke in the stairwell. Hands are shaken all around, and the firemen briefly pause to admire a nineteenth-century porcelain gentleman fondling a maiden in her cherry patch before rolling up their hoses and departing.

As round two of the election progresses, there is little respite from Le Pen's nightly harangues on TV, and a deep, ominous mood settles over the city. Gangs of skinheads and radical students appear in the streets. The more affluent citizens of Paris, ensconced in their chauffeured Mercedes sedans on the Champs-Elysées, begin to glance nervously through tinted glass. I am not surprised to read in *Le Parisien* one morning that a city businessman is auctioning off *Le Vulcain*. The extremely rare gem, carved from a single crystal and weighing 179 carats, is one of the world's largest black diamonds. It would seem that it is time to cash in one's chips and get out of harm's way.

The auction brought to my attention one of the world's largest strongboxes, located under the Crédit Municipal, or city pawnshop. The building itself hardly looks like Fort Knox. Spread over an entire city block, the nineteenth-century façade gives way to an open courtyard with a fountain at its centre. There are few signs of security, and clients can enter freely to pawn their household goods at the main office.

Underground, however, it is a different story. Over 1,300 square metres of storage space is guarded by steel gateways, personnel, and strongboxes that can only be opened with a combination of keys, security passes, and secret codes. It houses a vast store of private and corporate valuables ranging from Van Gogh paintings to diamond necklaces. In all, approximately eleven thousand objects rest within the coffers, with a total estimated value of at least 5 billion Euros.

Precious gems and dodgy scams, especially, have had an association with the Marais dating back to the time of the Sun King. The most famous case was "The Affair of the Diamonds," a delightful swindle that took place in the Hôtel de Rohan, an immense mansion that currently houses the national archives.

The hôtel was built for Cardinal Rohan, a rather vain and corpulent man with a crush on Marie Antoinette. He fancied her as a mistress, but she never had the slightest interest in him. In fact, word has it that she blamed the cardinal for a humiliating incident that occurred as she was travelling to Paris for her betrothal to Louis XVI. Stopped at the French border, she was made to strip naked and to remove everything that was of Austrian origin.

The focus of the diamond affair was a necklace crafted by the French jeweller Boehmer, who had unsuccessfully tried to sell it for 1.6 million francs to Louis XVI. Accounts of the affair are contradictory and full of claims and counterclaims. A popular version purports that Madame de la Motte Valois, a mistress of Cardinal Rohan's, fancied the necklace for herself and came up with a plan to acquire it using the gullibility and lecherousness of her lover. She forged a letter from Marie Antoinette to Rohan saying that she would look favourably on the cardinal if he were to buy this necklace for her.

When Madame de la Motte personally delivered the letter to the cardinal, he was naturally suspicious. He asked to meet Antoinette in person, so the crafty Madame arranged for a hot midnight assignation in the forest of Versailles with a prostitute disguised to look like the queen. Tantalized by this taste of forbidden fruit, the duped cardinal put the first payment down for the necklace and gave it to Madame de la Motte, who immediately broke up the necklace and sold the diamonds.

The subterfuge was soon discovered when the defrauded jewellers came looking for their second payment. When the truth emerged, the king had Cardinal Rohan stripped of his offices and sent into exile. Madame de la Motte was put in jail and branded with a V, for *voleur*, but the jewel thief later escaped to London where she had the last laugh, publishing a salty, vengeful memoir about court life in Versailles.

Perhaps the curse of the diamond affair rubbed off on *Le Vulcain*. In the end, the 1.2 million Euros minimum bid is not met, and the owner, whose identity is never revealed, is obliged to withdraw his gem from the auction. I doubt if he is sleeping any better at night.

As a distraction from the political hubbub, Linda and I decide to try a traditional French meal for dinner—horse meat. Although Monsieur Fontaine has a host of lamb, beef, and pork, one *viande* the butcher does not carry is deboned stallion. For that, I must go to a little store on rue Rambuteau. Technically, a horse butcher is called a *boucher chevalin* and advertises his wares with a bronze horse bust above the door. Monsieur Patin, however, opts for a more subtle window display, a green neon sign that flashes *Cheval*.

Entering the store, I make inquiries. Patin, it turns out, offers horse in two forms: *rumsteak* and *haché*. I opt for the rump steak and ask to have it trussed into a roast for the rotisserie in my oven.

"Where are you from?" inquires Patin. When I explain that I am Canadian, he informs me that my dinner is also Canadian, shipped all the way from Alberta. In fact, virtually all horsemeat in France comes from my home province. "Do you not have the *boucher chevalin* in Alberta?" he asks.

I have visions of kd lang foaming at the mouth at the very thought and assure him that we do not.

"*C'est pas normal*," he mutters, shaking his head at the irony.

When I get home, I am faced with another problem: what to serve with the meal? As far as I know, Betty Crocker never published anything on the subject, and the thirty-minute-meal recipes in the back of *Hello!* magazine tend to shy away from racehorse burgers. I am told that the meat tastes like beef, so perhaps some mashed potatoes and Yorkshire pudding would go well with Arabian. There are few wine books that recommend vintages for foal, but fortunately Bernard recommends a young Merlot that is perfect for the occasion.

As the roast cooks in the oven, I entertain a fantasy of

inviting unsuspecting guests over for the meal. I mentally invite Uncle Bert, a sanctimonious farmer from Saskatchewan whose chief form of entertainment outside Bible reading was goosing the local Chinese restaurant owner. "Golly, this is good," he exclaims sometime during his fourth helping. "What is it?"

"Saddle steak. Care for another helping?"

Alas, roast racehorse turns out to be less exotic than I had hoped, somewhat reducing its appeal in the vengeance department. One advantage I do note, however, is my sudden renewed interest in running. We live about half a kilometre from the Seine, a relatively short early morning gallop down rue Vieille du Temple. Some people might think that the drivers in Paris would make this feat all but impossible, but they are quite charitable toward anyone running down the middle of the road, either because they respect the insane, or because they think you've just robbed someone and are, therefore, armed.

The real danger to running in Paris is the kingpins, short metal poles painted black and topped with a solid steel ball precisely at the height of one's testicles. The city has placed these contraception devices every three metres along 5,000 kilometres of curb so that Parisians cannot park their cars on the sidewalk. The fact that it results in the occasional jogger castration is considered a side benefit.

I have another nit to pick regarding Paris streets: litter. I don't know why anyone would purposely sully such a beautiful city, but not a day goes by without the gutters becoming choked with soda cans, cigarette boxes, and fast food wrappers. Parisians say it is the tourists, but I know different. As I am returning from my run, I cross the pont de la Tournelle, just upstream from Notre-Dame. Ahead of me is a group of environmental activists carrying anti-fascist signs. "Keep French air pure, throw out Le Pen," says one. As they cross the bridge, a young man in skateboarder shorts and a Sorbonne T-shirt finishes off a bottle of Evian water, screws the top back on, and then flings it into the Seine. Not one of his comrades says a word. I suppress the urge to tuck a kingpin in his pocket and fling him off the bridge to retrieve it.

David calls and invites me to go to the massive flea market in Saint-Ouen. According to my guidebook, the neighbourhood started out at the turn of the century as a spot where itinerant merchants, banished by the authorities, set up a den of thieves just outside the city limits. While the market has grown to two thousand stalls spread over six hectares, it still retains much of that original spirit of enterprise. The quality ranges from (literally) heaps of junk to immaculate museum pieces—with a corresponding range of prices. Although bargains are few and far between, the flea market attracts up to 150,000 visitors each weekend in search of the perfect acquisition.

The *marché* is located in the suburb of Seine–Saint–Denis, which also has one of the largest concentrations of unemployment in France. Every weekend for the last few months, dozens of cars have been torched by bored, frustrated youths. When we arrive, the *marché* is already packed, and David is forced to park close to a large public housing estate, where he manages to squeeze into a tiny parking space by pushing a car forward a metre with his bumper. As we get out of his Rover, I silently hope David has fire insurance.

Gérard is in his shop, clean-shaven and dressed in a blue

blazer and neatly pressed trousers. His stock consists of marble-topped sideboards, glass-fronted display cases, and highly-polished *secrétaires*, all from the eighteenth and nineteenth centuries. When we arrive, he locks the front door of his shop, and we retire to the bar next door for a liquid lunch.

Gérard is the cheerful sort who enjoys the sound of his own voice. A glass of Alsace wine is all that is required to loosen his lips, and soon he is revealing the secrets of his trade. According to Gérard, the goal of all successful dealers is to find an antique that requires some work, but not *too* much work. He describes coming across a beautiful Louis XVI sideboard at an estate sale. The woman wanted 25,000 francs, a very reasonable price, but the piece had been left too close to a room heater, and a large section of inlaid wood had split and peeled off. "I would have to take it to the carpenter for repair, and he would have it for six months." Gérard waves his wine glass in the air, his index finger held aloft to underscore his point. "That is my money sitting there for half a year. One cannot afford to do that."

We finish our wine and bid Gérard adieu. David is searching for a candelabra to match the one he had purchased in the Vanves flea market the previous month. We wander through the major markets and out onto the back *marché*, where the owners of a long line of open-air stalls hawk clothing, drug paraphernalia, African masks, and surplus army boots. At the west end, we come to a huge warehouse filled with used furniture in various stages of disrepair. While I wander through rows of grungy gaming tables, cracked mantelpiece mirrors, and scuffed dressers, David strikes up a conversation with several of the burly stevedores sitting by the front door.

I have a theory that the fascination for other people's old junk stems from the fact that something that would normally be considered a revolting example of bad taste is lent respectability by age. I have almost walked right past what looks like a leather floor vase with a bad case of leprosy when I realize that it is, in fact, an umbrella stand made from the foot of an elephant. Some nineteenth-century Englishman obviously got it into his head that the pediment of a pachyderm would be the ideal repository for his brolly and promptly went on safari to bag one. I envision this poor elephant stumbling around the vast plains of Kenya on three legs and cursing Queen Victoria. I must have it.

My musings are interrupted by angry voices. I return to the front of the store where a very large man with a red face is poking his cigar in David's direction. "You don't know how dangerous it is around here," he yells. "I've had my car broken into and my shop robbed. It's crazy!"

We edge our way back out onto the street before things get too rambunctious. "What did you say?" I ask.

David puts on his most innocent face. "Oh, I just asked those guys who voted for Le Pen."

Both David and I are genuinely surprised by the spontaneous burst of anger unleashed by the shop owner. Most French citizens are more guarded in their comments, not wishing to express their feelings. Did others feel as resentful toward the presence of the immigrants, many of whom are refugees from civil wars in former French colonies of Africa?

I decide to ask Assam, a man who was born in Morocco but who has spent the last thirty years of his life in Paris, if he felt excluded from mainstream French life.

Assam, standing on the sidewalk in front of his florist shop on a busy Saturday morning, rubs the stubble on his chin before replying. "No. I am a French citizen and I have the right to vote. I have my work and I make a good living."

Has he ever been the victim of bigotry or prejudice?

"Discrimination is not a problem for me. My comportment is good with everybody."

Does he mix with other cultures?

"I have many Jewish and non-Jewish friends in the Marais. We have a good relationship—mind you, we don't talk politics or religion."

I am reassured by the florist's comments, but I still feel that there is much being left unsaid. I invite Pierre, a Frenchman who has spent several years in North America, to discuss this state of affairs over wine. After several glasses of Burgundy, the normally reticent man begins to open up. "If you want to know what a Frenchman fears, then ask him to tell you a joke." He gives me an example that is making the rounds in his social circle.

A little rabbit was sad because he woke up one day and forgot what he was. He was walking along through the field when a cow saw him. "Why are you so sad?"

"I forgot what I am."

"Oh, that's easy," said the cow. "You have long ears and a bushy tail, so you are a rabbit."

The rabbit cheered up instantly. He hopped along, a big smile on his face, until he saw a sad sheep. "Why are you so sad?" he asked.

"I have forgotten who I am," said the sheep.

"Oh, that's easy," said the rabbit. "You have short curly hair and you smell bad, so you are an Arab!"

Neither one of us laughs.

As much as the far right in France hates Arabs, the real targets for Le Pen's skinheads are the Jews. Schools and places of worship are attacked, including a synagogue in Marseilles that is burned to the ground by arsonists. A gang of disguised youths storm a soccer pitch and attack a team from a Hebrew school. Several children are injured before police arrive to chase the attackers away.

As the election progresses, the number of incidents increases until the Israeli minister of the exterior issues a blanket asylum to Jewish French citizens. The French government, stung by the insult, finally reacts. Overnight, the small number of police who have been guarding the rue des Rosiers in the Marais swells to a veritable brigade, with street barriers, armed patrols, and armoured carriers positioned night and day.

Walking down the rue des Rosiers, I spot a Middle Eastern restaurant specializing in falafels. In the window sit several trays of freshly chopped herbs and vegetables. Inside, the long, narrow room is crowded with wide leatherette booths, specially constructed to accommodate the well-padded bottoms of North American tourists. The walls are covered with celebrity photos of big-haired women. A portrait of a Rabbi, posted above the door, smiles down reassuringly upon the diners.

Benjamin, the maître d', is dressed in the staff uniform of a sleeveless T-shirt and three-day growth of beard. He greets me warmly and responds with great approval when I order the house specialty. He recommends a glass of carrot juice as the perfect accompaniment, but my gorge rebels at the thought of a glass of vegetable phlegm, so I opt for a Maccabee beer.

In the open kitchen near the front window, the chef reverses his baseball cap and gets down to culinary business. Slicing open a pita, he energetically loads in a bed of red cabbage, cucumber, lettuce, and onion before rescuing six tiny balls of crushed chickpea from the deep fryer and nestling them within. The concoction is then topped off with a spoon of yoghurt sauce, or something equally beneficial to my digestive tract, and served on a platter.

The sandwiches, as promised, are the best, and it takes all of my willpower not to order a second helping. I console myself with a generous helping of baklava pastry for dessert. By the time I am done, the restaurant has almost emptied, and Benjamin joins me for a coffee. His family, Tunisian immigrants by way of Israel, have lived in France since before he was born. When I ask if he is worried by the hatred stirred up by the election, he shrugs and stares out the window toward the street. "When this is all over, we'll still be here."

In the end, Le Pen polls less than 20 per cent of the vote, and Chirac celebrates a landslide victory, but the entire experience leaves the French battered, ashamed, and aware of the problems that deeply divide the country. "I don't think the people of France really are into the extreme right wing," explains Bernard, when I drop into his wine shop shortly after the election. "They didn't so much as vote for Le Pen as try to say that they weren't happy with what is happening to the country." He stops to think about all of the problems that the elite try to ignore, what the average Frenchman sees and experiences every day. "There are a lot of things that have to change, and there are a lot of things that will."

I am heartened by Bernard's optimism, but still skeptical. Would the average Frenchman give up his ingrained habits and embrace change? I am out strolling along rue Vieille du Temple pondering Bernard's words when I spy something even more rare in Paris than black diamonds—a tow truck.

From a North American perspective, it is very difficult to understand why there are no tow trucks in Paris. The streets are literally choked with abandoned cars. The police put wheel clamps on any vehicle that is parked illegally, but then they leave them sitting there for at least half a year. The owners, faced with humungous fines, simply remove the plates, pull the registration, and abandon the car.

So it is with great surprise, and not a little delight, that I suddenly spot a tow truck cruising down the street. Some things can change, I decide, including the sanctity of a Frenchman's car. I watch the driver pull to a stop at a loading zone where an irate grocery store owner is fuming over a tiny Fiat parked in front of his garage entrance. The car is wedged in between two other vehicles with less than seven centimetres clearance on either side. I wonder, not unreasonably, how the tow truck is going to get this car out of such a tight jam.

In answer, the driver lifts two metal dollies from the back of his truck. The devices are designed to slide under the back wheels of a car and then lift the wheels up off the asphalt. Once the dollies are locked in place, the tow truck operator simply pushes on the side of the car and the back end swings out onto the street. After he backs his truck up and lifts the rear end of the car, he stows the dollies and places two portable signal lights on the back of the vehicle. The entire operation takes less time than a pickpocket's pursectomy.

Unfortunately, it is not enough time for the car's owner to both get dressed and rush down to the street. A young woman wearing a man's shirt and a pair of sneakers, and very little else, bursts from a doorway and begins running down the street after the tow truck. "Hey! That's my car!"

The driver is so surprised by the appearance of a semi-clad woman in his rearview mirror that he actually pulls over and stops. The woman rushes to his door. "Please, let my car go! I'll pay the fine!"

The driver leans out the window and checks out her long, naked legs. "Where's your wallet?"

The woman suddenly notices the breeze. "Oops. I'll be right back." The driver watches her rush back to her apartment, then climbs out of his cab to disengage the car.

"How come you're letting her off the hook?" I ask.

He grins slyly at me. "What's the only instrument in an orchestra a man plays with his teeth?"

"I don't know."

He makes a motion of running a pair of thong underwear through his teeth. "The string."

And some things, I conclude, will never change.

JUIN

We are strolling in the Marais on a delightful Saturday evening, and the compass in my feet directs us toward the river. As we cross the pont Louis Philippe that connects Ile Saint-Louis to the rest of the city, a young couple is doing their best to perform mutual tongue flossing. Perhaps it is the sun setting over the Seine to the west or the sound of the bells of Notre-Dame carrying across the water, but a limpet couldn't be more firmly attached to the butt end of a shark compared to these two.

Parisians love to smooch anywhere in public, and you are just as likely to see them doing it in front of a laundromat as in front of a sunset backdrop. We once got on the #29 crosstown bus, which had a tiny open balcony on the back. Two students were standing there in such a wonderful embrace that we decided to do exactly the same, until a trailing motorist started to beep his horn and plant kisses on his windshield.

When amour strikes, even beggars get in on the act. I am walking down rue des Rosiers when I spot Jean-Pierre gazing into a jeweller's window. "*Ça va?*"

"*Ça va.*" Jean-Pierre shakes my hand, then points to a display. "What do you think of those sapphire earrings?"

"I think you'd look better in pearls."

"Very drole. This is not for me, it is for my sweetheart!"

I'm impressed. "Panhandling must be good these days."

Jean-Pierre takes on a pained expression. "I am not a pan-handler, I am *un homme d'affaires en plein air.*"

I suppose even outdoor businessmen get smitten by the bug. Frankly, I place the blame for all this on the water. As soon as warm weather hits Paris, the Eau de Seine, as it is charitably known, takes on a refined bouquet, something reminiscent of a ditch puddle in Delhi. Of course, anyone with any sense in Delhi drinks their water with a mix of gin, quinine, and lemon, but that doesn't seem to have caught on here. Other than a healthy dose of bromine supplied free of charge by the city fathers, you're on your own. The only sensible thing to do is drink wine, and lots of it. No wonder there's such a height-ened sense of amour.

Ardour in Paris, of course, goes much further than a few inno-cent kisses. While doing some research for a novel, I had the opportunity to call up a vice squad detective to ask his advice on the subject of love-for-rent. Which arrondissement, I asked, would be the most likely place to locate a house of prostitu-tion? The detective thought for a moment. "Is it a day whore-house, or a night one?"

Like the tides, it turns out that the carnality of the city has always had an incoming and outgoing rhythm. The day houses are located in the 1st arrondissement, where the butchers and greengrocers at the wholesale food markets in Les Halles would traditionally stop for a coffee and a piece of pie at the end of their work shift. The evening whorehouses are located near the Opera, so that Puccini lovers could savour an oral libretto before the main performance.

I make the mistake of bringing up this particular subject

during an evening tasting of Bordeaux in David's cellar, and he promptly decides to take us for a midnight tour of one of the most carnal spots in town. Driving west along avenue de la Grande Armée, he turns into the fashionable suburb of Neuilly-sur-Seine and heads south, until the art nouveau buildings along rue de Longchamps abruptly give way to the Bois de Boulogne. The bushes on the side of the road have been cleared back about ten metres to make room for red-clay bridle paths. Dense, dark forest looms beyond.

Just after we pass a large château, traffic slows to a crawl. I spot a woman in bright red, vinyl hot pants circulating between the cars, chatting with the men inside. Topless, she presses her large breasts against the windows and invites the men to step into the bushes.

"This," David announces, "is the transvestite hooker stroll. Can you believe it?"

We can't. Several dozen hookers, some in high-heeled boots and miniskirts, others in little else than a wig and a smile, proposition potential clients as they drive by. For the most part, they are young, pretty, and well-endowed. And when I say well-endowed, I don't mean just breasts. A black woman in red stilettos is more than happy to show off the toolkit in her thong.

As we roll along past the show, David explains that most of the hookers are a mix of Middle Eastern, Asian, and East European men who have gone through various stages of surgical and pharmacological enhancement. One way to pay for the expensive treatments is to solicit sex.

"Isn't prostitution illegal?" I ask.

"Pimping is illegal, but not prostitution." David points to the police standing around a paddy wagon parked on the verge. They are ignoring the goings-on and seem far more concerned with keeping order than nabbing johns in the middle of a blow job. There is a definite feeling of live-and-let-live to the festivities. David toots his horn, and several of the hookers wave gaily to us as we drive off.

A few days after our excursion to the Bois de Boulogne, an article in *Le Parisien* catches my eye. The Brigade for the Repression of *Proxénétisme* has finally put the cuffs on Madame Claude, an Englishwoman who has been operating a whorehouse with a stable of 452 call girls from a hotel just west of the Marais. Included in the story is a quote from the hotel manager. "We knew that the large, pretty brunette was some kind of a businesswoman, but he didn't suspect she was that kind. Although, when you think about it, she did know an awful lot of pretty young women." Now there's a man with a bright future in the tourism industry.

According to the police, Madame Claude, a graduate of the London School of Economics, used her business skills to set up an internet-based organization that accepted payment through a number of offshore accounts. Hiring the girls through modelling agencies, she charged them out at 1,000 Euros per hour (with a businessman's weekend special of 5,000 Euros), keeping 40 per cent of the proceeds. Her racket was finally run to ground when she refused to pay a local manager for back wages, and the unhappy hooker called the Paris police. Even jilted love, it seems, has its price.

Louis XIV is probably the most passionate man ever to have walked the streets of the Marais. His bronze statue stands in the courtyard of the Hôtel Carnavalet, one of the few life-size likenesses to survive the French Revolution. It shows the king in a Roman soldier's cuirass and a curly wig. Although he was short, at around 1.6 metres, and boasted that he had only taken three complete baths in his entire life, Louis made good on his goal to bed as many of his female subjects as possible. In addition to doing the horizontal mambo with One-eyed Kate, the Marquise de Montespan, and Madame de Maintenon, the king took a special fancy to Madame Soubise, wife of François de Rohan, Prince of Soubise.

The Madame was a red-haired beauty with delicate, pale skin, and her family understood the value of being the king's favourite. During their long-standing affair, she wore an emerald necklace to indicate to the king when her husband was away and the coast was clear. She had eleven children, and the fifth, who bore a striking resemblance to Louis, later became the Cardinal de Rohan. Eventually, the princess lost a tooth, and the king lost interest in her, but the largesse he bestowed was sufficient for the family to build the sumptuous Soubise Palace, a mansion so immense that it, along with the adjacent Hôtel de Rohan, now houses the majority of the six billion government papers comprising the national archives.

But it was Louis's lust for architectural erection that eventually ended the heyday for the Marais. The king spent millions of francs and worked for over forty years to create the most magnificent palace in the world, one that would impress not only the heads of Europe, but also the countless Asian tourists who came after. In 1674, Louis first took up residence in Versailles, and much of the nobility that lived in the Marais followed the king to his new home west of Paris.

We decide to make a similar pilgrimage, if only for a day. The last time we had been to Versailles, people were so tightly packed into the palace that it felt like the London Tube at 5 PM, only not as sweet-smelling. This time, however, we are able to stroll through the public galleries unimpeded. As we wander through the royal apartments, we admire the magnificent beds where the inhabitants could lay and gaze up at the ceiling frescoes of Greek gods chasing naked nymphs.

Louis had an immense area around the palace landscaped with canals, fountains, floral gardens, and forests. We walk for half an hour until we come to the Grand Trianon, a spacious château at the west end of the grounds. According to the guidebook, Louis would go there with his mistress every weekend to escape the crowds at Versailles. I note that several of the old goat's silk chaise lounges have a well-polished look to them.

Another thing I notice is that the park is incredibly clean. People in Paris have no hesitation whatsoever about throwing everything from cigarette packages to condoms into the gutter. Here, however, they go to great lengths to find a receptacle. I understand this is thanks to Louis, who led by example. For example, if he caught you throwing a candy wrapper into the canal, he would hang you. He was very progressive in many ways, but unfortunately the people of Paris didn't take kindly to his innovations and introduced Louis to their own novelty, the guillotine.

The following week, Jim, Linda, and I decide to attend another local institution—the evening show at the Moulin Rouge. The venue is located in Montmartre, along with about two-thirds of the world's triple-X-rated shops. The hall itself has a stage at one end, a floor of banquet tables in the middle, and a series of risers at the far end to accommodate the gawkers who just want a bottle of champagne and a decent peep.

We arrive after the meal has been consumed, which is a blessing, as the remains looked suspiciously like airline food.

The curtain rises, and a bevy of women come strutting out, each one dressed in traditional feather boas and sequined thongs. What makes a woman want to grow up and dance semi-nude in a chorus line? Do they, as ten-year-olds, disrobe their Barbies and listen to show tunes, fantasizing about the day they will don their high heels, remove their tops, and gyrate?

Regardless, they exhibit unfalteringly good humor, even the woman who hops into the glass-sided pool of boa constrictors that rises out of the stage floor. Several Japanese businessmen are not so sanguine, however, especially when a snake slides from its watery realm and makes a beeline for the left-over sushi. The management apologizes profusely and sends over a complimentary bottle of champagne, which, aside from dry cleaning some silk boxer shorts, is the least they can do.

I am sitting with Giorgio at a café on rue de Bretagne discussing the woeful state of European culture over a glass of wine. "I don't know art, but I know crap when I see it," he exclaims. "And Picasso is crap."

Picasso has been dead for almost thirty years, but few other artists still stir up as much fervour in Paris. Although he was born in Spain, Picasso's professional career blossomed in France. His legacy is scattered around the world, but the essence of his work is distilled in one building, the Musée Picasso, located in the Marais.

The Picasso Museum itself has a long and curious history. The massive, three-storey urban mansion was built by Pierre Aubert de Fontenay, a salt-tax collector. When it was finished in 1659, his neighbours took one look at the pretentious home and immediately nicknamed it the Hôtel Salé, or salty mansion.

Fontenay lived in his mansion just long enough for Louis XIV to have him arrested and thrown in the Bastille for embezzlement. Through the centuries, the home passed through several owners until it was finally reclaimed by the state. As Picasso neared his death in 1973, the French government enacted special legislation that would allow his heirs to avoid estate taxes by donating the artist's private collection to the state. When Picasso passed away, the government received over a thousand paintings, drawings, and sculptures. On any given day, several hundred works are on display, including many of his famous Cubist paintings. Maybe it's because I don't know what crap is, but my favourite work is a simple, abstract head of a bull, sculpted from the seat and curved handlebars of a bicycle.

I am on my way home from my Tuesday afternoon lunch with Giorgio, musing on his words. It is a hot, sticky day, and I follow the shade of the tall buildings along rue de Turenne, the local centre for Jewish tailors and haberdashers. The clerks in one wholesale men's wear outlet have removed the pants from the mannequins in the window display. They stand there in button-down collars and silk ties, white, plastery legs sticking out from beneath shirt-tails, slightly embarrassed but no doubt cooler for their plight.

As I round a side street onto rue Vieille du Temple, I bump into a man who introduces himself as Pablo Picasso. This particular version hails from somewhere in equatorial Africa and has a distinct love for Johnny Walker, but otherwise appears to be the same in artistic spirit. At night, Pablo sleeps in an alleyway, and in the day he gathers together materials and sets up a studio near his museum, where he specializes in a mixed medium of effluvia, paint, and whiskey.

I stop to admire one of his works, a large canvas to which

he has affixed an advertising poster featuring a caricature of a black man savouring a popular banana-flavoured drink. Much of the poster is obscured by a thick layer of white wash, as is the surrounding sidewalk. Pablo has completed the composition by nailing several old Nikes to the surface with some tacks and the butt end of his liquor bottle.

"You like it?" asks Pablo.

"I do." Try as I might, I can't quite get the metaphor, but the effect starts to grow on me, like a warm fungus.

Pablo rubs his lips with the back of his hand. "It's yours for a bottle of scotch."

I check my pockets, but, sadly, I'm all out of single malt. I change the subject and ask the artist about the large bump on his forehead. Teeth flashing in a grin, he tells me he got it while riding in the undercarriage of a jet that flies from Dakar to Paris. I laugh, thinking he is pulling my leg. Later, I read in *Le Parisien* about a corpse found in a forest north of the city. Alerted by hikers, the police had recovered the body of a man, apparently of African persuasion, stuck in a tree on the approach to Charles de Gaulle airport. Some artists will do anything for inspiration.

When the Senegalese soccer team flew to Seoul to play France in the first match of the World Cup, they decided to fly there inside the plane, with obviously beneficial results. Normally, I have about as much interest in soccer as I do in Polish wine, but when we arrive at the Jardin du Marais restaurant for dinner that evening, more out of politeness than curiosity, I ask the maître d' who had won the game that afternoon.

"I do not think it was France," she replies.

Ooh-la-la. France had, in fact been beaten by Senegal, a

tremendous upset for the previous world champions. It was as if Japan had trounced the United States at Olympic basketball, only worse. France lives and dies by the efforts of its team.

By the following morning, Paris is in turmoil. The red, white, and blue banners hanging around the city suddenly take on the look of funeral bunting. "What has happened to our *Bleus*?" scream the newspaper headlines. Pundits fulminate on TV. "Are our boys too well paid, too pampered? Have they forgotten the reason why they're there?" In cafés, much breast beating of the male sort erupts. "How could they lose to Senegal? *C'est pas normal*! If they lose one more game, *sacré*, they will be eliminated in the first round."

Bernard, as always, is sanguine. "They always lose the first one," he assures me. "They just want to generate a little excitment."

Les Bleus generate a lot more excitement later in the week when they tank in spectacular fashion against Uruguay. The stirring chords of the Marseillaise have hardly fled the air when a French defender commits a vicious foul and is ejected from the game. After that, the French team are playing at a distinct disadvantage, and even though they have no trouble thwarting the Uruguayan forwards, their superb attackers are turned back time and time again. The game ends in a scoreless tie.

A deep despair settles upon the land. Soufflés go flat, baguettes hang limp, and even champagne loses its fizz. The French are examining their soul, and it is no time to waste one's passion on mere food and wine. What has happened? Are we lost?

One faint hope remains: Zinédine Zidane. The team's star forward is coming back from injury for the next game. Surely the world's greatest player can pull *Les Bleus* from the abyss.

A large screen has been set up in the public space in front

of the Paris Hôtel de Ville. On Tuesday morning, I go down to watch the third match, between France and Denmark. As I walk down rue Vieille du Temple, the bars and cafés are crowded with remarkably pious people, their hands clasped together in prayer.

By the time I arrive at the Hôtel de Ville, five thousand people have already congregated in the open space, mostly teenagers, but also a sprinkling of businessmen in suits and families on an outing. In between shouting at the kids in front to sit down, a petite, red-haired mother with two teenage daughters explains to me that the French have to win that day or they will be eliminated. "And that would be terrible, Monsieur," she assures me.

The referee's whistle blows, and a tremendous roar arises from the crowd: *Allez les Bleus!* Unfortunately, it is the Danish who respond and score the first goal. The mood of the crowd starts to turn ugly. When a Danish player fouls a French defender and receives a yellow warning card, I laugh derisively at his protestations of innocence.

The red-haired woman turns to me. "What, you think this is funny?"

What I distinctly don't think is funny is 5,000 Frenchmen wondering if I'm wearing Danish boxing shorts. "No! I want *Les Bleus* to win!"

As the match winds down through its closing seconds, the French coach puts out all his attackers in the vain hope that they can score one goal. Instead, the Danish respond with a second marker, and a huge groan of defeat runs through the crowd. "Too little, too late—*merde*," mutters a pinched-face clerk. The red-haired mother, her head hanging low, hugs her daughters and walks slowly from the square. The riot police, stationed behind city hall in case of a victory, stand down.

The media aren't so sanguine. "Twisted and blinded by success and money, the players and those around them neglected the most important thing: the soccer field," whines *Le Figaro*. *Le Parisien* takes a dig at both *Les Bleus* and Jospin, their favourite whipping boy prior to the World Cup. "The principal error was ignoring the first round and preparing exclusively for the final phase, like those who were preparing for the final phase of the presidential race."

When I go to see Bernard at the wine shop, he barely glances up from his task of storing wine boxes. "I couldn't care less," he mutters. "It's just a game—there's more to life than football."

Every morning I like to start my day with a fifteen-metre dash down the spiral staircase to the front door of our apartment, not because I am athletically inclined, but to prevent my newspaper from being inundated.

Precisely at 7:47 AM, the sound of a poorly-tuned diesel engine infiltrates our living room from the street below. It is the deliveryman for the *International Herald Tribune*, stopping briefly to kick my paper under the front door. Usually at this time of the morning, I am sitting on the living room love-seat, drinking my first coffee and slowly joining the light of day.

Until the water truck turns the corner, of course. At 7:53 AM, the large municipal vehicle, equipped with a water jet attached to the front bumper, swings onto rue Barbette and proceeds down the street. All manner of debris—cigarette butts, dog excrement, and candy wrappers—is swept away by a powerful blast of water.

Unfortunately, the large gap below the front door is at

precisely the right angle to allow the water to squirt several metres into the foyer. At the sound of the truck, I leap up from the couch and race down the rickety stairs to rescue my paper from a soggy demise.

For those who think Paris is gripped by endless strikes, it may come as a surprise to hear about the effectiveness of those who provide public street services. They are not only punctual, but also conscientious. Every morning, just before the water truck arrives, a man in a lime green jacket appears with a green plastic twig broom. He picks up pop cans and other objects, then uses the broom to push dog piles off the sidewalk. After the water truck has passed, he pauses to smoke a cigarette in an ivory holder and to peruse the pristine street, satisfied with a job well done.

This professionalism extends to garbage pickup. Every building is equipped with a large green plastic bin in a cubby hole near the front door in which residents deposit their kitchen scraps and apartment detritus. Every evening at 6 PM, the *gardien* wheels the bin out front, and precisely one hour and seventeen minutes later, an immense garbage truck inches around the corner and empties the bin.

And, when there is a change of schedule, they let you know by posting flyers. Linda is returning from work when she spots a sheet of paper that has been stuck to the bin: "Exceptional Notice! Due to the *Fête de la Musique*, collection on June 21 will occur at 5:30 PM. You are advised to place your trash out no later than 5:00 PM. Thank you very much, Your Garbagemen."

I am intrigued. They don't even do early collection on Christmas Eve. What, pray tell, is the *Fête de la Musique*?

"Oh, it's a great awful bloody noise," explains Nigel, our neighbour. "It's a bunch of street musicians sawing cats."

Nigel's wife, Margaret, is more generous. It is, she explains, a free music festival that celebrates the summer solstice. "It's the most wonderful night of the year."

On 21 June, *Le Parisien* comes complete with a pullout section listing the festival events throughout the city. There are over fifty in our neighbourhood alone, ranging from twelfth-century choral chants in the place des Vosges to a group called Urgu that promises an evening of Stockholm punk and ethno, Swedish buffet included. By the time Linda returns home in the early evening, an Urgu sound technician is booming "CHECK, CHECK," through a 50,000-watt amplifier, apparently intent on broadcasting the concert to Mars. Jim arrives shortly thereafter with Gwen. After a glass of wine, we unanimously decide it would be preferable to get as far away as possible from Urgu before they blast off.

As we walk down rue des Francs-Bourgeois, the strains of other, more celestial music comes to our ears, first from an African drummer pounding out a song from Mali, then from a classical string quartet playing Vivaldi's *Four Seasons* in the courtyard of the Musée Carnavalet.

By now, drivers on rue des Francs-Bourgeois have given up making any headway against the sea of humanity that is flooding the centre of the street, except for a taxi driver who hops out of his cab and starts shouting at the top of his lungs. "Hey! Some people have to make a living around here! Get out of my way!" He persists until a shirtless young man wearing Doc Martens and Satanic tattoos offers to dance on his roof.

We stop at a brasserie located at the corner of rue des Francs-Bourgeois and rue de Turenne. Our waiter, who has pomaded his hair like Elvis's for the occasion, escorts us to a table overlooking the street. Over a pitcher of Brouilly and plates of rare steaks, we watch an endless stream of Parisians—single mothers pushing their children in strollers, white-haired seniors, teenagers with pierced belly buttons—all making their way toward the nearby place des Vosges. Finishing our meal, we soon join them.

The wide street circumscribing the place des Vosges is jammed with several thousand people. A large crowd stands at the nearest corner singing along as a crooner belts out Yves Montand ballads. Farther along, two sopranos have set up shop beneath the arched colonnade and are singing a Mozart aria, their voices echoing from the warm stones and bathing the audience in the glow of their song. Our favourite group is a classical orchestra stationed near Victor Hugo's residence; with an assortment of violins, cellos, and harps, they work their way through several Beethoven pieces.

We leave the place des Vosges and head west along rue de Rivoli. It is dark by now, and the traffic along the normally busy thoroughfare has been displaced by tens of thousands of revellers heading for the Hôtel de Ville to hear a Franco-Caribbean lineup of techno DJs. Along the way, a busload of German tourists stares out in disquiet at the shouting throng. Why are they dancing? Is this some sort of Gallic riot? From the look on one man's face, he couldn't decide whether to film the scene or to make out his will.

We are sidetracked by an improvised barbecue stand on rue Vieille du Temple. Two transvestites in backless evening gowns are dancing on a rickety wooden table and waving a sign: *saucisse*. Their cohort, a beefy man hovering over a portable cooker, is obscured by a thick white plume of smoke created by the grease from four dozen chorizo sausages. We pass on the *saucisse* and instead purchase a round of ice-cold Japanese beer.

Thinking that a little live entertainment might be in order, we wander up rue du Bourg Tibourg, toward the Lizard Lounge. The Liz, situated below a Turkish bathhouse, is well-known for its total disregard for the city's noise laws, and has also been cited under various sections of the bylaws for public lewdness. This, we all agree, is an excellent recommendation.

The evening is taking on a haze not overly conducive to objective reportage, but we generally conclude that the Liz is living up to expectations. A temporary stage has been set up at the front, and a man wearing a cowboy hat and a G-string is happily gyrating to the house band, Gun Blast Rock'n'Roll. Above, a group of muscular, shirtless men lean out the windows and call down invitations to whomever catches their fancy.

The gyrating dancer is joined by two performers of uncertain gender in red latex, and the trio demonstrates a suggestive dance move that meets with general approval from the crowd. Several police officers are invited to join in, but they point out quite rightly that the strenuous steps might set off their cans of pepper spray.

Even though the Liz promises to party 'til 4 AM, we have had enough jollity for one night. In a few hours, the street sweepers will be out to clean up the debris. In the meantime, we make our way home before anyone can get around to sawing a cat.

FIN

The hot, muggy weather that grips Paris at the beginning of July sucks the energy out of everyone like a 136-kilogram mosquito does, so I am not too surprised when Linda arrives home from work on Monday afternoon wilted and beat. I am dismayed however when a frosty glass of *Crémant de Loire* fails to revive her spirits.

"What's wrong?"

"The project's been cancelled."

We had suspected our days in Paris were numbered, but instead of bracing for the ax to fall, we had been deluding ourselves into thinking that, somehow, the companies in charge of Linda's project would pull through with an extension. There's no finer opiate than delusion, I guess. We spend the rest of the evening re-calibrating our senses with wine in a vain attempt to regain the shores of reality.

"We could hang out in St. Tropez until something else comes up," I offer.

"Good plan—I'll macramé owls, and you can sell strawberry crepes on the beach."

One of the nicest things about being laid off, of course, is that you can drink champagne and orange juice for breakfast on Tuesday, which is what we are doing when Jim arrives at our house the next morning. He is definitely feeling somewhat dejected by the decision and just wants to hang out at the family cabin in Manitoba for a little while. In spite of our entreaties, he is adamant, and we are somewhat dispirited to see that even he is abandoning Paris. Perhaps, we decide over our vitamin-laced bubbly, we can change his mind next week, during the project-demobilization party.

The party is the brainchild of David, who has discovered a disturbing surplus in the company's entertainment budget. He has convinced Christian, the manager, to hire a riverboat for an evening cruise on the Seine. Having seen the cavalier way cruise boats navigate under the narrow bridge arches, I find the concept somewhat disturbing, but David is adamant that everyone will have lots of fun. And if they don't, I suspect, at least he will enjoy throwing them overboard.

The weather is clear and mild when we arrive at the marina adjacent to the Palais Omnisport Bercy. The *Jonah*, not the most propitious name, is a flat-bottomed riverboat with a large, glass-walled party room outfitted on its deck. The kitchen is situated aft, where several moribund fish are floating on top of the water. Do they know something I don't?

David is late, so Christian greets the twenty-four guests personally as they come on board. When David finally does arrive, he immediately heads for the hors d'oeuvres table and digs in with both hands. "Man, I'm starving," he announces. "Let's get this show on the road." The captain swings the *Jonah* smartly into the central waters of the Seine, and we are swept downstream by the current, toward Ile Saint-Louis.

For most of recorded history, the Ile Saint-Louis was a low slug of mud peeking above the waterline like a clay crocodile. One man's sludge is another man's gold, however, and during the seventeenth century, developers reinforced the banks with stone berms and built a bridge to the right bank. Vagrants were ousted in favour of the rich and affluent. It is still known locally as "the millionaires' island," and residents speak of going to "the mainland" when crossing over to shop. Thanks to tourism, however, the island is currently taking one in the shorts. Every three minutes or so, a tour boat floats by and blinds the inhabitants by pointing its immense floodlights up toward the old stone mansions. I suspect more than one resident yearns for the good old days when you tossed the contents of your *Bourdaloue* out the window into the river below.

As we sail under the pont Louis Philippe, the setting sun hangs suspended between the twin belfries that dominate Notre-Dame's façade. For a second, I can imagine myself as a fourteenth-century boatman, my eyes rising from the toil of rowing to gaze upon this magnificent structure. Mind you, I'd be keeping an eye out for chamber pots, too.

The sun has set by the time we reach the Eiffel Tower, and the entire structure is lit by thousands of lights. My enjoyment of this vision of light is somewhat dampened by the chanteuse, who serenades us with the theme song from the movie *Titanic*. Someone's got a black sense of humour, don't they?

Heading back upstream, we take the south passage directly beneath Notre-Dame. From that perspective, the flying buttresses resemble spidery legs, and the cathedral takes on the appearance of a giant limestone arachnid creeping its way toward the water. Amazing what a little change in angle and a whole lot of Chablis will do to your perception.

When we reach the safety of the quay, the chanteuse turns the entertainment duties over to a DJ, and the tiny dance floor is soon full of bodies gyrating to an eclectic mix of cheesy disco and Lebanese rock tunes. The first mate demonstrates her prowess with the belly dance and we party into the early morning, finally exiting the boat and wending our way into the cool night air.

Jim still wants to return to Canada and spend the rest of the summer feeding mosquitoes. Linda and I can't bear the thought of going home, so we tentatively make a decision to try and stick it out in Paris, in the hope that some new situation might arise. After much counting of pennies and returning of pop bottles, we estimate that we may be able to hang out in the city until the end of the summer.

Our one big worry is our utility bill. Electricité de France and Gaz de France offer the efficiency of state control with the friendliness of a bureaucracy, all at monopoly prices. Not that anyone looks forward to utility bills, but after going a year without receiving any notice at all, we are more than a little concerned about what our charges might be mounting up to. We contact Monique, the estate agent, who promises to look into our dilemma.

About two weeks later, we receive a copy of a notice from Electricité de France detailing the charges over the course of the year. According to Monique's calculations, we owe almost 3,000 Euros. My eyes bug out like twin golf balls at the sight; how could we possibly use up 3,000 Euros of energy in just one year? The 5.5-metre neon windmill over the Moulin Rouge doesn't go through that much juice.

There is also the matter of the gas. As far as I can tell, the stovetop in our kitchen is the only gas appliance in the house. I dig out a flashlight and go in search of our gas meter in the hallway. I find it hidden behind an ancient panel in the stairwell, about halfway up to the next floor. I scrape off a thick pile of dust and try to read the number. Sure enough, we have managed to use enough gas to fill the Hindenberg. What the hell is going on?

Just then, Monsieur Greco ascends the steps, a baguette tucked under one arm. "*Ça va?*"

"*Ça va bien, merci.* I am trying to read this stupid meter."

Monsieur Greco shakes his head in sympathy. "Ah, the gas. It is very expensive, no?"

"*Oui!*" I show him the bill. "Can you believe it?"

"*Ooh-la-la.* Your home must be very hot."

"What do you mean?"

"The heating—it is all on the gas, no?"

Come to think of it, there are some rather immense, hot radiators in every room. "Do you have a gas heater in your home?"

"Of course."

"Is your bill this large?"

Monsieur Greco glances up and down the stairwell to ensure that we are alone. "Perhaps it could be there is only one meter for the entire floor."

"You mean I'm paying the Maestro's, too?"

Monsieur Greco holds his hand out flat, palm down, and shakes it like a small fish. "Anything is possible."

I thank Monsieur Greco and go back inside. It makes sense—why would the Maestro put in two hot water heaters, when one would do for the whole floor? All I can think about are the windows left open for a week in January. No wonder the bill's so high, we're keeping the entire Marais warm. We send off a note to Monique, noting in a polite but firm tone that we refuse to pay the heating bill for the neighbourhood.

About a week later, there is a knock at the door. I open it to discover a young man standing at the portal with our note in his hand. "You sent me this?"

The man looks vaguely like the Maestro, but a good thirty years younger. Boy, are they ever getting good at facelifts these days. I'm thinking of getting one myself when he explains that he is Pascal, the Maestro's son, and it is now his responsibility to take care of the flat.

I try to sound indignant. "I don't think it's right that we should have to pay all the gas and electricity."

Pascal nods in agreement. "No, I don't think it's fair. What do you think you should pay?"

My brow furls. What is this, some kind of Gallic trap? Hah, I'll turn the tables on him. "What do you think I should pay?"

Pascal shrugs. "How about one-third. Is that fair?"

If it's a trap, it's a damn good one. "I can live with that, but only if we make an agreement in writing."

Pascal smiles broadly and agrees. In spite of the hot weather, it's beginning to look a lot like Christmas.

The *chaleur* finally lets up on Bastille Day, and the morning arrives cool and overcast with a hint of rain. Linda and I are jogging down rue Vieille du Temple, heading for the Seine, when we hear thunder in the distance. Only it isn't thunder. The sound rolls up and down the narrow street, getting louder and louder, until five jet fighters streak low overhead, their afterburners emitting trails of red, white, and blue smoke. By the time we reach the Seine, a full military fly-by is in progress. Attack helicopters, cargo transports, and supersonic jets rumble down the river one after the other. It's too late to go down to the Champs-Elysées to catch the rest of the parade in person, so we turn and head for home, hoping to see it on TV.

Every July, French media are full of dashing accounts of the French Revolution. The storming of the Bastille on 14 July

1789 marks the official beginning. Contrary to popular belief, however, the prison was not attacked and destroyed as a symbol of royal repression. True, it held prisoners behind its walls at the king's pleasure, but the fortress was far better known for its wine cellar than its dungeons.

What the Bastille did have in abundance was ammunition, a commodity highly prized by the citizens of Paris. Ever since the citizens' parliament had convened in Versailles two months earlier, the delegates had been under constant threat from the 30,000 troops stationed by Louis XVI around Paris. Country peasants, driven into the city by a food shortage, were also rampaging through the city, attacking bakeries and food stalls. Not surprisingly, the townspeople had formed a militia of 48,000 men to protect their homes and families. But with only picks and axes to arm themselves, there was little they could do.

At sunrise on the morning of 14 July, the militia gathered at the gates of Les Invalides. Behind its walls lay 32,000 rifles— enough to arm the citizen army. The governor in charge refused them entry, but sympathetic war veterans housed within the confines of the wall unlatched the fortified gates and let the protestors in. They soon found themselves in possession of the arsenal without a shot being fired. The reason for that bloodless victory soon became apparent; there wasn't a single ball or charge of gunpowder in the Hôtel. Where could they find ammunition? "*A la Bastille!*"

The Marquis de Launay, governor of the Bastille, was in the habit of touring his fortress after breakfast. When he mounted the wall that morning, he was alarmed to see thousands of decidedly unhappy drapers, wine merchants, and gardeners milling about below. A delegation stepped forward from the mob and demanded he hand over the ammunition; the marquis refused. Although the garrison numbered only one hundred men, they were secure against an unarmed mob behind the high walls and deep moat. He immediately sent word to the city's governor, the Duke of Orleans, to dispatch reinforcements.

Unknown to the marquis or the militia, two men had climbed atop a perfume shop adjacent to the walls of the Bastille and snuck into the tower beside the main gate. Using axes, they cut the chains and lowered the drawbridge. The mob, thinking that the marquis had capitulated, rushed into the central courtyard. The surprised Launay ordered his men to fire. Caught in the trap, scores of unarmed men were cut down. The mob retreated, shouting treachery. News of the massacre raced through town, and the angry crowd around the Bastille swelled ominously.

By 5 PM, events at the fortress had come to a head. A regiment of the king's guards mutinied and joined the protestors, bringing along four cannons. "Give up!" they demanded. Instead, Launay threatened to ignite the sixteen tons of gunpowder in the arsenal, blowing up the Bastille, the mob, and much of the Marais.

Not surprisingly, Launay's men considered this a very bad idea. Bayonets in hand, they requested he come up with a better plan. The governor finally gave in, surrendering his garrison on the condition that they spare his men. Exultant, the mob rushed in and released the seven prisoners. Once they were in possession of the Bastille, however, the mob took its revenge, ransacking the fortress, drinking wine from the cellar, and killing Launay.

In rather purple prose, the British historian Thomas Carlyle describes the reaction of Louis XVI in his epic tome *The French Revolution* (1832). The king had just retired for the night when word reached Versailles. His master of the robes, the Duke of Liancourt, informed him of the capture of the Bastille.

"This is a revolt!" said Louis.

"No, sire," responded the duke. "It is a revolution."

Now, why can't I think up good lines like that?

By the time we arrive back home, most of the military parade along the Champs-Elysées has already marshalled past the review stand in place de la Concorde, and it is time for the Cuisine Corps to present arms. The men, dressed in floppy white chef hats, salute their *chef du command* with egg-beaters.

"*Magnifique*," intones the announcer.

The Second Logistics Brigade appears next, their huge bulldozers and bulletproof water trucks emblazoned with a rather bellicose looking yellow pelican on a field of herring. I can only think there must be a very interesting explanation for the logo, but the announcers are surprisingly mute on the subject. Whatever the reason, I'm sure it's a real conversation-starter whenever the lads drop in to the bar for a few pints.

The last to pass is the Presidential Republican Guard, two hundred men mounted on horseback, red and black feather boas hanging proudly from each of their gold helmets. I immediately forget the pelican. Who did the Guard hire to design their uniforms? LaCroix? It is precisely at this moment that an assassin, a right-wing fascist known to the police, tries to shoot President Chirac, but misses badly. It turns out that the Guard's uniforms distracted his aim.

Thinking that the French in general have a fine reverence for explosives, we set out that night to watch the annual fireworks display held near the Eiffel Tower. Jim had warned us that it is best to avoid the crowds that gather on the Champs de Mars, so we agree to meet on the pont des Arts, near the Louvre.

By dusk, the clouds have cleared and a quarter moon hangs over the National Assembly. From our position at the railing, we can see the top half of the Eiffel Tower. Beneath us, tour boats, floodlights ablaze, make their way downriver. Across the way, in the 6th arrondissement, the illuminated façade of the Académie Française glows in autocratic splendour.

Around a thousand people have gathered on the pedestrian bridge to watch the show. A group of young men and women on a blanket beside us munch on a picnic of pizza, Pringles, and Camembert cheese. A brass band arrives, and that traditional French melody, "The Lion Sleeps Tonight," soon floats over the river. The tuba player, wearing a Jimi Hendrix wig, is so impressively bad that the audience doesn't know whether to laugh or throw him off the bridge.

Right at the stroke of 10:30 PM, the lights on the Eiffel Tower go out and the show commences. We crack a bottle of champagne, the cork slicing a delicate arc through the air until it lands on the waters below.

That proves to be the aerial highlight of the evening. Most of the fireworks are hidden below a low row of apartments on the far bank, and the noise of the explosions carries upriver as a series of dull thumps. Fortunately, the more champagne we drink, the better the band sounds, and we are glad we didn't throw them off the bridge. By the end of the evening, everyone is dancing to a rousing version of "Tequila!" This is definitely something the Académie should look into.

One of the tiny, but perfect luxuries of Paris is Berthillon ice cream. Throughout the Marais there are shops that sell the confection during the summer months, a circular scoop of heaven in a sugar cone. My favourite is *cacao*, a dense, almost fudgelike chocolate. Linda and I purchase a cone on Ile Saint-Louis, then stroll across to the pont de la Tournelle. An artist has set up his easel on the sidewalk of the bridge and is intent upon capturing Notre-Dame cathedral in the post-impressionist, pre-Gothic, pseudo-vampirish school of art currently sweeping Paris. He is wearing a thick leather coat in spite of the fact that it is hot enough to roast chestnuts on the hood of your car. Holding up his right thumb, he sights down his arm to get the true perspective that one can only achieve using a grubby digit, then applies several confident dabs of acrylic paint from tubes randomly plucked from his coat pockets.

I note that he is embellishing Notre-Dame with a line of palm trees, and snicker. The *artiste*, overhearing me, sneers and points. True to his vision, a dozen palm trees have sprouted adjacent to the building—nine-metre trees with masses of long fronds sprouting from the top.

And they are moving. Not swaying, but *moving* at a slow, but undeniable, speed. I rub my eyes, but the hallucination persists. Mother told me this would happen if I drank enough French red; inanimate objects would start to move and eventually sing Barry Manilow tunes. I began to glance nervously about for lounge acts when Linda saves my sanity.

"That must be the Paris *Plage*."

Every August, the mayor of Paris closes the Georges Pompidou highway adjacent to the Seine to allow pedestrians and other bipeds the privilege of strolling along the river unimpeded. This year, as a special treat, he has spent more than one million Euros of taxpayers' money to create an artificial beach, complete with sand, umbrellas, and palm trees imported from Cannes.

We wander down to take a closer look. The shoulder of the road has been lined with sand, and in place of hubcaps and wine bottles are rows of lounge chairs upon which Parisians nurture their carcinomas. Nearby, a *pétanque* pit, complete with an obligatory beer and cigarette booth, is doing roaring trade as players roll steel balls back and forth on the clay surface.

Just east of the *pétanque* pit is a gaping hole in the steel guardrail that is supposed to keep cars from plunging into the river. Right beside it stands a signboard intriguingly entitled "Secrets of the Seine." Scurrying over, I am disappointed to discover that the "secret" that the sign reveals is the river's abundant fish population, including bream, eel, and lobster. Who cares about that? I want to know what caused the big hole in the guardrailing. Was it a running gun battle between some Marseille mobsters and the police? Was Scarface Louis sleeping with the mud carp at this very moment?

My thoughts are interrupted by a young man gliding serenely past on roller skates. He is wearing a kilt, a sequined sporran, and a yarmulke. He is, no doubt, on his way for a kosher pint at the gay Scottish pub on rue François Miron. I just love the way Parisians get into the spirit of things.

Faced with repatriation to the United States, David has decided to make the best of it and open up an antique shop in Dallas. It's a backup plan, he explains to Pam, just in case Americans stop burning gasoline in their Jeeps, and he's out of a job. Since Pam refuses to go flea marketing anymore, David invites me to visit his favourite antique shop, located in the heart of the Saint-Ouen flea market.

The shop is run by Sophia, who lives in a real château out-side Paris with her husband and young daughter. While David snoops around, Sophia sells a set of Italian, nineteenth-century wooden stands to Billie, a well-preserved antique dealer from Austin, Texas. I help Billie carry the stands outside into the sunshine for a better look. The hand-carved wooden pedestals stand about 1.2 metres high and feature cherubs and demon faces. One of the pedestal surfaces has a minor crack, but Billie is unperturbed. "You don't want too much damage, but it has to have *some* damage, Honey," she explains in a deep, throaty growl. "Ain't nothin' lasts hundred years without damage." Her work done, she ambles off in search of a Bourbon to gargle.

In the meantime, David has fallen deeply in acquisition lust with a circular breakfast table of creamy marble and inlaid travertine, complete with four matching upholstered chairs. He asks the price. Sophia, like a true *brocanteuse*, still works in old francs. She has listed it for 30,000 francs, but offers it to David for 25,000.

David gives her that ol' aw, shucks look. "I'll give you 20,000. That's 30 per cent off."

"Thirty per cent off is 21,000," says Sophia.

"Oh." David tries a different tack. Pushing on the seat of one of the chairs, he shakes his head. "These seats don't look too good. I think I'll have to re-spring them." I happen to be sitting on one of the chairs. "How does it feel?"

"They're very comfortable."

"No! That's not what you're supposed to say!" David turns back to Sophia. "The material looks a little worn. I'll probably have to get them re-upholstered. Right, Gord?"

"They look great to me."

David slaps his head. "This is the last time I bring a Canadian along antique shopping."

I suggest he go over and check the tabletop. "Maybe it has some damage."

David is happy to comply. "Hey, this has chips off the edge!"

"That's because it's *old*." Sophia places her hand on a large wooden mallet resting on a side table, and I get the distinct impression she wouldn't mind taking a few chips out of David's noggin. They haggle for another few minutes, but David sticks to his price.

"I'm Lebanese and I'm only going to pay 20,000."

Sophia crosses her arms. "I'm Protestant and I'm only going to accept 21,000."

Finally, David agrees to Sophia's price. "But only on the condition you deliver it, and if it's damaged by the delivery men, I'm not going to buy it."

"Agreed."

It is 3 PM, and business is winding down at the market. David, high from another acquisition, jams the chairs from the dining set into the back of his Range Rover. "My wife's gonna kill me." He waves happily to Sophia and turns his car for home.

It is our last night in Paris, and almost by instinct, we wander down to the Seine and stand on the pont Louis Philippe. A warm breeze is trailing up the river as the bells of Notre-Dame strike their evening chords, the sound echoing off the massive silhouette of the Hôtel de Ville.

I think about going home. Soon, we will be back in our apartment overlooking the Rocky Mountains. In the mornings, we can go for bike rides along the Bow River and, in the evenings, sit out on the balcony and share a glass of wine with our friends, telling them all about our time in the Marais.

But as much as I am excited about going back, I hate leaving Paris. This is no sterile, interchangeable North American city, but a glorious assault on the senses. I begin to think about all that I will miss.

The olfactory bouquet alone is worth a sonnet. It isn't just the attractive smells—the fragrance of roses on a hot day, the aroma of onions frying in butter in Camille's kitchen, the perfume wafting behind a young woman as she walks up the street—but all of the scents that adorn Paris. I think of cold, wet chestnut leaves rotting in the gutter, the damp black earth awaiting tulip bulbs in the Musée Carnavalet garden, even the sour vapour of urine that hangs in the Châtelet Metro station. It is all part of me now.

I will miss the visual images that Parisians delight in creating. Everyone knows that when you stand at the Louvre and gaze up the Champs-Elysées, the outline of Napoleon's Arc de Triomphe fits precisely into the Grand Arch at La Défense. And the city abounds with such architectural delights. Whenever you walk across the pont Louis Philippe toward Ile Saint-Louis, the dome of the Pantheon looms on the Left Bank. Through a trick of perspective worthy of a magician, it grows to immense dimensions as you traverse the narrow street leading south across the island, until you finally come out to the open expanse of the south channel, and the dome suddenly shrinks to less stupendous dimensions.

Some of the visual treats are so tiny they are easy to miss. There is a hardware shop window on rue de Poitou that has been decorated in a riot of puns—hammerhead sharks and swordfish swimming over a coral reef covered with clam(p)s. Along rue Vieille du Temple, bakers display immaculate, symmetrical rows of glazed raspberry tarts against a border of pure white meringue. The grocer on rue Rambuteau spends hours polishing and positioning oranges, green apples, and lemons to create a display brighter than a circus tent.

I will miss the sounds: the chorus of church bells peeling forth on Easter Sunday, the garbage truck trundling up the street at 7 PM every evening, even the kid who customized his scooter muffler with a hacksaw.

I will miss the food: *chausson aux pommes* pastry with a *café crème*, fresh baguette in Madame Garcia's bakery, the scores of wines that never make it beyond the shores of France, fresh white asparagus in butter and lemon, and cherries hand-dipped in chocolate.

I will miss the people of Paris: Jean-Pierre and his goofy grin, Assam and his flowers, Miam–Miam and the other waiters at Camille's.

But mostly, I will miss living for the moment. As I've mentioned before, in North America, the day is spliced into a pre-packaged series of episodes, everyone isolated into their car, their mall, or their suburban box. Here, when you walk out the door, you never know what you're going to encounter: plum blossoms, riot police, or freshly baked bread, still hot from the oven. Each day springs to life as a full-blown performance, and if you are not part of the audience, you are part of the cast.

We lean against the bridge railing one last time, clasping each other and staring out over the city. Can it get any better than this, I wonder? Seeing us, an accordion player stops on the bridge and begins playing "La Vie en Rose," the sweet, sad melody floating up into the night air above us. It can, I conclude.

Our final day at rue Barbette dawns with a clear blue sky. We drink our coffee as we listen to the sounds of the awakening street below, the gush of the water truck mixing with the greetings between neighbours as they walk their dogs.

The flight is scheduled to leave before noon and we don't have much time. Returning to the kitchen, Linda cleans out the coffee maker, washes the cups, and places them back onto the shelf beside the stove, there to await the next tenants. I close the windows in the living room and begin to draw the curtains shut when I suddenly stop. I go to the front door and grab my jacket off the coat rack.

"Where are you going?" asks Linda.

"There's something I have to do. I'll just be a minute." I run down the twisting lanes until I reach the Saint-Paul Metro station; Jean-Pierre is sitting in his usual spot. A big grin spreads across his face when he sees me.

"Hey, Canada!"

"Hey, Jean-Pierre." I pull out a 10-Euro note. "This is for you."

Jean-Pierre's eyes go wide as he instinctively reaches for the bill, then his hand stops in mid-air. "What is this for? Do you want me to buy some new clothing?"

"No."

"Food?"

"No."

His brow furrows in suspicion. "What, then?"

"I want you to put it on a horse."

Jean-Pierre takes the bill from my hand. "Which one?"

"You know the one."

Jean-Pierre winks as he shakes my hand. "*Bais, oui*. I know the one. Good-bye, Canada."

"*Au revoir*, Jean-Pierre."

I turn and walk away, my heart as light as crème brûlée. It's just another Paris moment.

ABOUT FIFTH HOUSE

Fifth House Publishers, a Fitzhenry & Whiteside company, is a proudly western-Canadian press. Our publishing specialty is non-fiction as we believe that every community must possess a positive understanding of its worth and place if it is to remain vital and progressive. Fifth House is committed to "bringing the West to the rest" by publishing approximately twenty books a year about the land and people who make this region unique. Our books are selected for their quality, reader interest, saleability, and contribution to the understanding of western-Canadian (and Canadian) history, culture, and environment.